macOS Daemonology

Communicate with Daemons, Agents, and Helpers Through XPC

Volodymyr Vashurkin

Apress®

macOS Daemonology: Communicate with Daemons, Agents, and Helpers Through XPC

Volodymyr Vashurkin
Dnipro, Ukraine

ISBN-13 (pbk): 978-1-4842-7276-3   ISBN-13 (electronic): 978-1-4842-7277-0
https://doi.org/10.1007/978-1-4842-7277-0

Copyright © 2021 by Volodymyr Vashurkin

Managing Director, Apress Media LLC: Welmoed Spahr
Acquisitions Editor: Aaron Black
Development Editor: James Markham
Coordinating Editor: Jessica Vakili

Distributed to the book trade worldwide by Springer Science+Business Media New York, 1 NY Plaza, New York, NY 10014. Phone 1-800-SPRINGER, fax (201) 348-4505, e-mail orders-ny@springer-sbm.com, or visit www.springeronline.com. Apress Media, LLC is a California LLC and the sole member (owner) is Springer Science + Business Media Finance Inc (SSBM Finance Inc). SSBM Finance Inc is a **Delaware** corporation.

For information on translations, please e-mail booktranslations@springernature.com; for reprint, paperback, or audio rights, please e-mail bookpermissions@springernature.com.

Apress titles may be purchased in bulk for academic, corporate, or promotional use. eBook versions and licenses are also available for most titles. For more information, reference our Print and eBook Bulk Sales web page at www.apress.com/bulk-sales.

Any source code or other supplementary material referenced by the author in this book is available to readers on GitHub via the book's product page, located at www.apress.com/978-1-4842-7276-3. For more detailed information, please visit www.apress.com/source-code.

Printed on acid-free paper

I owe much to those who have contributed to the software developer in my soul.

Writing this book, I have a heart full of gratitude to:

- *Apress team, who inspired me to write this book*
- *Sergii Teteriuk, my teacher who helped me become a programmer years ago*
- *the Apriorit company in person of My first tutors, Roman Mokych and Eugene Kordin, for showing me the right vision from the beginning*
- *Oleg Kulchitskyi for his assistance in my wandering through the Darwin Kernel*
- *my parents, Olga and Alexander, who gave me love, unique personal qualities and showed me the way of software development.*

"Have the courage to follow your heart and intuition. They somehow know what you truly want to become."

—Steve Jobs

Without Steve's passion and technologies, this book couldn't exist. Thank you and rest in peace.

Table of Contents

About the Author

Vladimir @alkenso Vashurkin loves the macOS system as well as security development and research. Why macOS? He says, "The first two weeks of developing under macOS were hell. The following seven-plus years were heaven."

Vladimir started system and security programming while researching FileVault full disk encryption on macOS and its interaction with iCloud. iCloud uses plenty of system daemons and user agents, so his investigation of Apple's infrastructure gave him a solid understanding of how the background world works and piqued his interest in system programming.

Besides system programming, the Darwin kernel and kernel development also found their place in Vladimir's heart. During his work, Vladimir has faced plenty of tricky cases, lack of documentation, and minor and major documentation mistreatments and wants to help people make sense of it all.

In the personal background world (i.e. real world) Vladimir likes extreme sports such as snowboarding, wakeboarding, and motocross. In 2020 he found the best kind of personal transport: the electric unicycle. He loves traveling and exploring the beauties that Mother Nature has gifted us.

About the Technical Reviewer

Mezgani Ali is a PhD student in transmissions, telecommunications, and artificial intelligence (National Institut of Postes and Telecommunications in Rabat) and a researcher at Native LABs. He likes technology, reading, and his little daughter Ghita. His first program was a horoscope generator in Basic in 1993, and he has done a lot of work on the infrastructure side of system engineering, software engineering, managed networks, and security.

Mezgani has worked for NIC France, Capgemini, HP, and Orange, where he was part of the Site Reliability Engineer (SRE) team responsible for keeping the data center's servers and customer applications up and running. He is fanatical about Kubernetes, REST API, MySQL, and Scala and is the creator of the functional and imperative programming language PASP.

Mezgani has a master's degree in mathematics and computer science from the Research of Superior Institute of Science and Technologies in France; he has a bachelor's degree in engineering from XXX in Morocco.

Mezgani is a serious, modest, and relaxed person, and he's always looking for ways to live life by constantly learning new things to improve himself.

PART I

Daemons in a wild

Disclaimer: most of the examples and mentionings of macOS as a system with open access to the file system, processes, etc. At the same time, all other devices of the Apple family (running by iOS, watchOS, ...) have almost the same internals.

The book could be treated as developers' manual for macOS and as researchers' guide for the rest of Apple OSes.

Disclaimer 2. All examples and materials of this book are relevant up to its publishing date.

All information is actual for macOS BigSur, Xcode 12 and Swift 5 language.

CHAPTER 1

Operating System Background World

In this chapter, we'll explore the operating system background world, comparing what OS shows to the user to what is actually going on behind the scenes.

Behind the Scenes

What do users see when looking at the desktop while doing their jobs?

Most of the time we see nice, shiny applications with rich and pretty interfaces.

These applications may have a single window or multiple ones (Figure 1-1). They show graphics, get user input, and provide output using attractive animations and bright colors.

© Volodymyr Vashurkin 2021
V. Vashurkin, *macOS Daemonology*, https://doi.org/10.1007/978-1-4842-7277-0_1

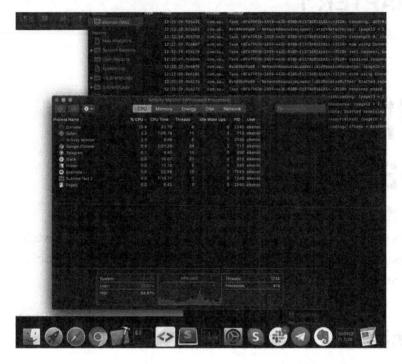

Figure 1-1. *Applications visible to the user (macOS 11.0)*

But how do they work? How are they launched? How do they interact
with the system? How does the system itself manage those apps and their
windows?

All the typical user knows is that the system has a kernel side (where
the device drivers reside) and a user side (where the final applications
run). See Figure 1-2. But there is also a huge and important workhorse
connecting these two worlds in a secure operating system called *daemons*.

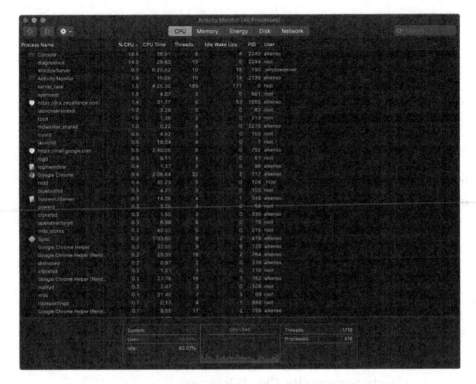

Figure 1-2. *Visible and background applications (macOS 11.0)*

Who Are the Daemons?

Now, a daemon is not the same as a demon. According to historical information, a *daemon* is a kind of creature designed by the gods to perform various kinds of work that the gods themselves do not want to do. This terminology was first used in the so-called Maxwell's Daemon.[1]

In the operating system world, *daemon* is the common name of the process running in the background. (In Windows, they are called *services*.)

---

[1] https://ru.wikipedia.org/wiki/%D0%94%D0%B5%D0%BC%D0%BE%D0%BD_%D0%9C%D0%B0%D0%BA%D1%81%D0%B2%D0%B5%D0%BB%D0%BB%D0%B0

Daemons are

- Designed to be closer to the OS interaction rather than the user interaction

- Running in the background

- Usually deprived of any windows/GUI

Every OS including macOS has dozens of daemons that perform all the internal operating system work. Here are some examples of daemons on macOS:

- fseventsd: Writes file system event log files and monitors file system changes.

- mds: Stands for "metadata server" and is part of Spotlight.

- securityd: Maintains security contexts and arbitrates cryptographic operations and security authorizations.

- cloudd: Supports the CloudKit feature.

- sharingd: Used by the Finder to enable AirDrop file sharing, connecting to shared computers, and accessing remote disks on other computers.

- bluetoothd: Manages all the Bluetooth devices and Bluetooth communication.

- VTDecoderXPCService: A sandboxed host used by QuickTime for video and audio decoding.

As you can see, there are plenty of daemons that do various tasks.

Note   You can view all the daemons and agents registered on your Mac.

Simply run `launchctl list` in Terminal to list the user agents for the current user and run `sudo launchctl list` to list the system-wide daemons (see Figure 1-3).

```
                        alkenso — -sh — 80×24
Alkensos-Mac:~ alkenso$ launchctl list
PID     Status  Label
-       0       com.apple.SafariHistoryServiceAgent
-       0       com.apple.progressd
3469    0       com.apple.cloudphotod
360     0       com.apple.Finder
361     0       com.apple.homed
400     0       com.apple.SafeEjectGPUAgent
-       0       com.apple.quicklook
-       0       com.apple.parentalcontrols.check
-       0       com.apple.PackageKit.InstallStatus
452     0       com.apple.mediaremoteagent
523     0       com.apple.FontWorker
385     0       com.apple.bird
-       0       com.apple.amp.mediasharingd
-       0       com.apple.familycontrols.useragent
```

Figure 1-3. *Example of different daemons registered in the system*

For more information, see Chapter 3.

Now let's talk about why there are so many daemons and why macOS needs all of them.

Why Do We Need All These Daemons?

There are many reasons to create and use different daemons. Probably the most significant are shared functionality, functional separation, permission separation, and stability.

Shared Functionality

Daemons are stand-alone processes, which means they may have state or provide some specific functionality.

So, it is a common practice to keep some specific functionality in the daemon and interact with it from different applications.

For example, a daemon implements the core logic of the application. Also, the application has a user-visible main app, a background agent to show notifications, and a command-line tool to run specific commands via Terminal (see Figure 1-4 and Figure 1-5).

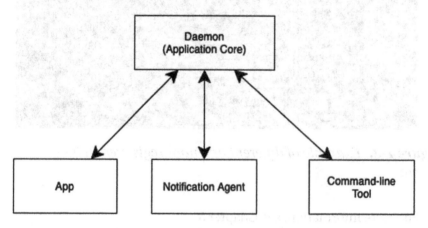

Figure 1-4. *Example of sharing functionality using a daemon*

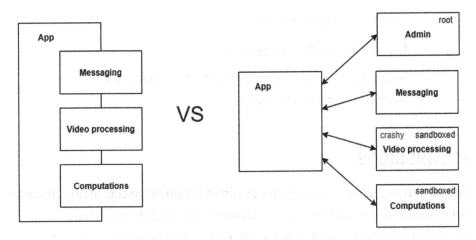

Figure 1-5. *Splitting an application into the application + multiple daemons*

Specific Functionality

Daemons of different types can perform functions that are complicated (or impossible) for the usual user-oriented apps:

- OS launching and bootstrap
- Security checks
- File activity monitoring
- Network activity monitoring
- Task/process management

As additional example, the following product types utilize daemons for their specific needs:

- Custom servers like HTTP, FTP, SSH, and SMB
- VPN (root access to network functions)
- Antivirus (root access to the file system and resources)
- System monitoring

9

- – User login/logout actions

- – Enterprise privilege management

- – Menu bar items (show icon/notifications when the main app is not launched)

Permissions

Different types of daemons of are permitted for different sets of operations. Root daemons (usually called just *daemons*) are eligible to perform administrator-level operations. User daemons (called *user agents*) run in the user session. They have no elevated privileges, but instead are capable of showing some GUI elements for users (such as notifications and menu bar items) that are still working in the background. Some daemons may be sandboxed to restrict their access to the outer world.

See Figure 1-6 for an example of privilege separation.

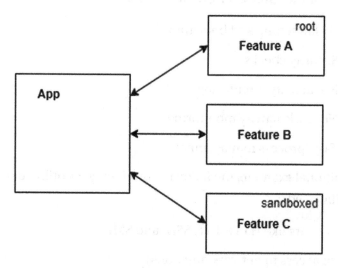

Figure 1-6. Permission separation

EXC_BAD_ACCESS: App Crash vs. Connection Lost

Of course, we all write perfect code. It never crashes and does not upset our users.

However, let's assume somewhere we have a defect in our code, leading to the application crashing (see Figure 1-7).

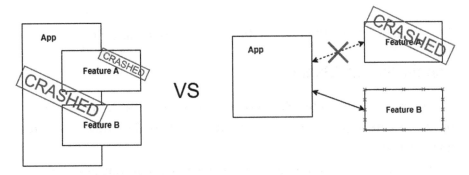

Figure 1-7. *Improving stability using daemons*

In the case of the "classic" monolithic approach to an application, the user loses everything at once when an application crashes.

But when taking out parts of the code and putting it into individual services, the worst thing is the connection loss, and the user will lose only one feature. An application even may show a nonfatal error and relaunch the service.

Of course, this approach complicates the architecture of your application. But what is a little complexity over huge benefits like crash-safety?

Going Out of Kernel

Sometimes special needs require us to deal with the kernel.

The most important rule of kernel development is this: move as much as possible out of the kernel (see Figure 1-8).

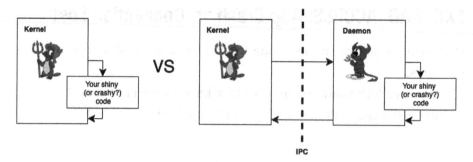

Figure 1-8. *Moving logic out of the kernel into the daemon*

Keep the System Stable

Kernel development is complex and risky: missing an issue in the usual app crashes the app, but missing an issue in the kernel module causes the entire OS to crash.

One of the popular approaches is to move as much code as possible out of the kernel into the daemons, usually with root privileges.

Here, daemons come to the rescue. Running as root, they communicate with the kernel module, receive raw input, process it, and send processed data back to the kernel.

Even if the daemon crashes, it means only the process crashes, keeping the rest of the OS stable.

Keep the System Secure

The main rule is to run with elevated privileges with the least amount of code possible." And that makes sense especially when you develop in kernel mode.

Having a lot of code leads to a higher probability of exploitation of holes left unseen by the developers.

Leave the kernel code as simple as possible and place complex things into usermode daemons.

Don't think that this is inefficient: Apple heavily utilizes this technique and introduces dozens of daemons-processing requests from the kernel and sends back results.

System-Managed Lifetime and Options

In contrast to applications usually launched and exited by a user action, a daemon's lifetime is controlled by the operating system (see Figure 1-9).

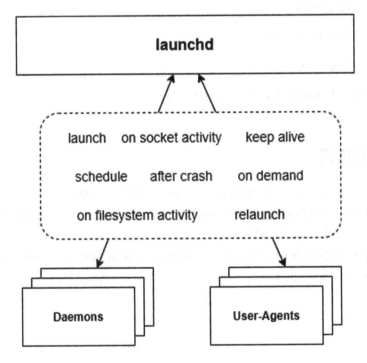

Figure 1-9. *launchd responsibilities*

Depending on the daemon settings, a daemon can be launched/relaunched in the following situations:

- On system start/user login

- In the case of a crash

- On demand by an XPC call

- On some schedule

- When a device is mounted

- When the file system path has been modified

Also, the daemon's settings allow you to specify limits and restrictions on the following:

- CPU time

- Memory usage

- File usage

For detailed options, see // TODO: add ref.

Summary

This chapter gave you an overview of daemons, first-class citizens of the operating system background world. Also, we looked at why and how daemons can be used and for what purposes.

In the next chapter, we will look at the daemon's anatomy and see what the daemons actually are.

CHAPTER 2

Daemon Anatomy

This chapter explains the anatomy of the daemons: what they consist of, what properties they have, and where they reside in the file system.

Also, the chapter provides an example of a simple daemon that you can write and run yourself in five minutes.

What Is the Daemon?

A daemon is a plist file (job description).

A daemon in the *OS operating system family is represented by a config file (`.plist`) with a description of the daemon and the executable to run. Daemons are run under `launchd`.

Note   In this book, the term *daemon* is used to mean the pair-specific configuration plist and executable unless another meaning is explicitly given.

To run under `launchd`, you must provide a configuration property list file for your daemon. This file contains information about your daemon. Specifying this information in a property list file allows `launchd` to register and launch your daemon immediately or on demand.

A daemon has a configuration file in property list [1] format. The typical daemon configuration contains such required and recommended keys as described in Table 2-1.

© Volodymyr Vashurkin 2021
V. Vashurkin, *macOS Daemonology*, https://doi.org/10.1007/978-1-4842-7277-0_2

Table 2-1. *Most Common launchd Configuration Plist Keys*

Key	Description
Label	Contains a unique string that identifies your daemon to launchd. (Required.)
ProgramArguments	Contains the arguments used to launch your daemon. (Required.) Note: May be replaced with the Program key specifying the path to the executable instead of an array of arguments.
KeepAlive	This key specifies whether your daemon launches on demand or must always be running.
RunAtLoad	This key specifies whether your daemon launches when loaded or should run only on-demand.
MachServices	This optional key is used to specify Mach services to be registered with the Mach bootstrap subsystem. Each key in this dictionary should be the name of the service to be advertised. The value of the key must be a Boolean and set to true. Alternatively, a dictionary can be used instead of a simple true value.

Let's look at a simple example of the built-in system daemon called cloudd that resides in /System/Library/LaunchDaemons/com.apple. cloudd.plist (Listing 2-1).

Listing 2-1. cloudd Daemon Configuration Plist Example

```
<?xml version="1.0" encoding="UTF-8"?>
<!DOCTYPE plist PUBLIC "-//Apple//DTD PLIST 1.0//EN" "http://
www.apple.com/DTDs/PropertyList-1.0.dtd">
<plist version="1.0">
```

```
<dict>
    // Array of arguments to run the daemon's process.
    <key>ProgramArguments</key>
    <array>
        <string>/System/Library/PrivateFrameworks/
        CloudKitDaemon.framework/Support/cloudd</string>
        <string>--system</string>
    </array>
    // Label that uniquely identifies the daemon to launchd.
    // 'service-name' in terms of launchctl.
    <key>Label</key>
    <string>com.apple.cloudd</string>
    // Mach services to be registered as XPC endpoints for this
        daemon.
    <key>MachServices</key>
    <dict>
        <key>com.apple.cloudd.system</key>
        <true/>
        <key>com.apple.cloudd.system.cache-delete</key>
        <true/>
    </dict>
    // Other configuration keys.
    <key>POSIXSpawnType</key>
    <string>Adaptive</string>
    <key>EnablePressuredExit</key>
    <true/>
    <key>EnableTransactions</key>
    <true/>
</dict>
</plist>
```

Placement

The property list file is structured in the same way for both daemons and user agents. You indicate whether it describes a daemon or agent by the directory you place it in. Property list files describing daemons are installed in LaunchDaemons directories, and agents are installed in LaunchAgents.

Where you place the executable file doesn't matter at all because this is just the path in the Program/ProgramArguments section of the configuration file.

Table 2-2. *Daemons Placement on File System*

Location	Description
/System/Library/LaunchDaemons	Apple's system-wide daemons
/Library/LaunchDaemons	Third-party system-wide daemons provided by the administrator
/System/Library/LaunchAgents	Apple's per-user agents installed for all users
/Library/LaunchAgents	Third-party per-user agents installed for all users (provided by administrator)
~/Library/LaunchAgents	Third-party per-user agents installed only for the current user (provided by the current user or administrator)

The difference between global user agents and local ones is that the global agents will be associated with all users of the OS. Local or user-specific agents are associated only with a specific user.

Note   Root privileges are required to put an agent in a global scope.

Daemons placed in .../LaunchAgents are also called *user agents*. User agents are launched under the concrete user with the corresponding user privileges.

Daemons placed in .../LaunchDaemons are called just *daemons*. Daemons are system-wide and are launched as root.

An important note here is that daemons (root) are system-global and run in the single instance under the root for the whole system. It runs as if no users are logged in or even if multiple users are logged in at the same time.

User agents instead are launched per user. So, there is a normal scenario running multiple user agents launched under different users.

Exercise

In this exercise, we will create our very first daemon configuration file.

In further exercises, we will evolve it and see how to register it, manage it, and communicate with it.

First, we need to create a simple executable that will be run as a daemon process.

At the moment, it will simply log information about its startup.

Also assume that the daemon's executable will be placed on the Desktop (see the value for the Program key in Listing 2-2).

Note The daemon will be written in Swift as the main language promoted by Apple. Please consider running it only on macOS 10.15 or newer, because these OSs have full runtime support for Swift.

In general, the daemon may be written in any language. The single requirement is that it should be a valid executable for macOS.

Executable - VeryFirstDaemon

Note   You can find this code at `// CODE: Daemonology/ 1-VeryFirstDaemon`.

Listing 2-2. Demo Daemon Executable

```
import Foundation

NSLog("Daemonology: the very first daemon has pid
\(getpid()).")

RunLoop.main.run()
```

Configuration plist file - com.daemonology.veryfirstd.plist

Listing 2-3. Demo Daemon Configuration Plist

```
<?xml version="1.0" encoding="UTF-8"?>
<!DOCTYPE plist PUBLIC "-//Apple//DTD PLIST 1.0//EN" "http://
www.apple.com/DTDs/PropertyList-1.0.dtd">
<plist version="1.0">
<dict>
        <key>Label</key>
        <string>com.daemonology.exercise_1.testd</string>
        <key>Program</key>
<!--    Place the daemon to the Desktop for test purposes.-->
<!--    Full path (without tilda) is required.-->
        <string>/Users/alkenso/Desktop/testd</string>
        <key>RunAtLoad</key>
        <true/>
        <key>KeepAlive</key>
        <true/>
</dict>
</plist>
```

To start the daemon, do the following:

1. Place the daemon's executable on the desktop.

2. Change the `Program` argument in the `configuration.plist` file to the exact place of the daemon (in the example, I've mentioned the `Desktop` folder for my user).

3. Place the daemon's `configuration.plist` somewhere.

4. Bootstrap the daemon:

   `launchctl bootstrap gui/501 /path/to/com.daemonology.`
   `veryfirstd.plist`

5. See the record about the daemon start in `Console.app`.

Daemon Bundle

When people talk about the daemons, they usually mean just an executable that is run as a daemon.

As we can observe on system daemons, most of them are plain executables placed inside frameworks or in `/usr/bin/libexec`.

But making daemons plain executables applies some restrictions on them like the following:

- Impossible or complicated signing with specific entitlements + provision profile

- Hard to deliver linked against custom frameworks/dylibs

- Hard to deliver with related resources

All these limitations may be avoided by making daemons as the usual
`.app` bundle! Regardless of whether our daemon runs as user or root, it still
can be bundled.

Placing the daemon inside the bundle solves all the problems
described earlier. That is handy to keep all the dependent resources and
frameworks along with the daemon.

This approach eliminates problems with packaging and deploying
daemons. It allows Swift daemons to embed Swift frameworks if they are
deployed on macOS versions older than 10.14.4 (those OSs have no Swift
runtime libraries installed on the system by default).

Create a skeleton for a bundled daemon by following these steps:

1. Create the usual App target.

2. Delete UI-related files such Asserts, in
    `xibs/storyboards`.

3. Leave a single `main` file in your daemon's startup
    code.

4. Do not forget to place `Runloop.main.run()` at the
    end of the daemon's `main` to prevent the daemon
    from exiting when the main thread work is done.

Note   You can find this code at: `//code Daemonology/`
`2-BundledDaemon`.

---

launchd

In *OS systems there is a "special" daemon named launchd that is an
analog of the `init` UNIX-like systems.

launchd always has PID 1 (PID 0 is a kernel itself).

The following are the main tasks of launchd:

1. Initialize the system.

2. Start/restart the processes.

3. Daemons support.

4. XPC support.

launchd has been open sourced up to 10.9.4.[1]

An interesting fact is that launchd has a personal Twitter: @launchderp.[2]

launchd is a bootstrap and service management daemon.

launchd has two main tasks. The first is to boot the system, and the second is to load and maintain services

When you turn on your Mac, launchd is one of the first things launched, after the kernel. This is why launchd has a process ID (PID) of 1, on every Apple OS (kernel_task has a PID of 0).

The launchd Startup Process

After the system is booted and the kernel is running, launchd is run to finish the system initialization. As part of that initialization, it goes through the following steps:

1. It registers system-level daemons from the property list files found in /System/Library/LaunchDaemons/ and /Library/LaunchDaemons/.

2. It registers the sockets and file descriptors requested by those daemons.

3. It launches any daemons that are requested to be running all the time.

---

[1]https://opensource.apple.com/source/launchd/launchd-842.92.1/
[2]https://twitter.com/launchderp

4. As requests for a particular service arrive, it launches the corresponding daemon and passes the request to it.

5. When the system shuts down, it sends a SIGTERM signal to all the daemons that it started.

The process for per-user agents is similar. When a user logs in, launchd does the following:

1. It registers each user agent from the property list files found in /System/Library/LaunchAgents, /Library/LaunchAgents, and the user's individual ~/Library/LaunchAgents/.

2. It registers the sockets and file descriptors requested by those user agents.

3. It launches any user agents that are requested to be running all the time.

4. As requests for a particular service arrive, it launches the corresponding user agent and passes the request to it.

5. When the user logs out, it sends a SIGTERM signal to all of the user agents that it started.

launchd can launch daemons in any order. If a request comes in for a daemon that is not yet running, the request waits until the target daemon finishes launching and responds.

Developer note   This behavior may cause unpleasant scenarios such as the following:

- The process P sends a request to the daemon D.

- D is not launched, so `launchd` launches it.

- For some reason, the executable file for D is missing.

- P waits for a response from D indefinitely.

The solution for such a situation is to set a timeout for the first calls to the daemons. If time runs out, just invalidate the connection.

CHAPTER 3

Daemon Management

In this chapter, we'll see how to set up and manage daemons. We will discuss the launchctl tool in detail. We will also cover the Swift API to compensate the lack of an official API from Apple for daemon management.

The Main Tool: launchctl

According to the man page, launchctl is an interface tool used with launchd to load and unload daemons/agents and generally control launchd. With it, you can do the following:

- Register daemons.

- Enable and disable daemons.

- Get information about daemons.

- Get information about the launchd session.

launchctl Terminology

Service is just another name for a daemon. It also may be called a *launchd job* or *bootstrap job* in different docs.

© Volodymyr Vashurkin 2021
V. Vashurkin, *macOS Daemonology*, https://doi.org/10.1007/978-1-4842-7277-0_3

The service name is what is specified in the plist file for the `Label` key. The service name uniquely identifies the daemon. Here are some examples:

- `com.apple.cloudd`

- `com.apple.sharingd`

- `com.apple.syslogd`

The domain target is a namespace for services, and each namespace has specific behaviors associated with it.

Table 3-1. *Daemons domain-targets*

Domain Target	Description
`system`	Targets the system domain. The system domain manages the root services and is considered a privileged execution context. Anyone may read or query the system domain, but root privileges are required to make modifications.
`gui/<uid>`	Targets the user domain for the given UID. A user-login domain is created when the user logs in to the GUI.
`pid/<pid>`	Targets the domain for the given PID or a service within that domain. Each process on the system will have a PID domain associated with it that consists of the XPC services visible to that process, which can be reached with `xpc_connection_create(3)` / `[NSXPCConnection initWithServiceName:]`.
`user/<uid>`	Targets the user domain for the given UID. A user domain may exist independently of a logged-in state of the user.

(continued)

Table 3-1. (*continued*)

Domain Target	Description
login/<asid>	The same as gui/<uid>, but uses the ASID token instead of the UID.
session/<asid>	Targets the session domain for the given audit session ID or a service within that domain. For more information about audit sessions, see auditon(2) and libbsm(3).

Note   For everyday tasks only the system and gui/<uid> domain targets are used.

The following service target is the identifier that uniquely identifies the service. It consists of the domain target and service name:

<domain-target>/<service-name>

Here are some examples:

- system/com.apple.cloudd

- user/501/com.apple.sharingd

Basic Interface

The following commands are listed in the style of how they are most commonly used. Some of them may have an extended or alternate form of invocation. Please refer to [3] for a full description.

boostrap <domain-target> <paths ...>

The paths can be plist files, XPC bundles, or directories. Each plist or bundle is loaded into the specified domain.

Listing 3-1 shows an example.

Listing 3-1. *launchctl Bootstrap Example*

```
// Register system-wide daemon that will run under the root
with specified configuration.
sudo launchctl bootstrap system /Users/alkenso/Desktop/com.
daemonology.veryfirstd.plist

// Register user agent (daemon that will run under the used
with uid 501) with specified configuration.
// Command succeeds only if the caller has uid 501.
// Otherwise, it should be invoked with 'sudo'.
launchctl bootstrap gui/501 /Users/alkenso/Desktop/com.
daemonology.veryfirstd.plist
```

This unloads the specified service:

```
bootout <service-target> | <domain-target> <paths...>
```

Listing 3-2 shows an example.

Listing 3-2. *launchctl Bootout Example*

```
// Deregister system-wide daemon.
// By configuration path:
sudo launchctl bootout system /Users/alkenso/Desktop/com.
daemonology.veryfirstd.plist
// Or by label:
sudo launchctl bootout system/com.daemonology.veryfirstd

// Deregister user agent using label (service-target).
sudo launchctl bootout gui/501/com.daemonology.veryfirstd
```

Warning!   Be careful. The paths are actually optional; you can unload an entire domain, which you probably should not do.

Developer Note   When bootout the job, launchctl time to time exists with status code 36 "Operation is in progress". Honestly speaking, for years of development it always means "Success" and nothing else. Consider handling this status as success in your code or scripts that invoke launchctl. You can also see all launchctl status codes in Listing 3-3.

This marks the service as runnable (or not):

```
enable <service-target> | disable <service-target>
```

Once a service is disabled, it cannot be loaded in the specified domain until it is once again enabled. This state persists across boots of the device. This subcommand may target services only within the system domain or the user and user-login domains.

This allows you to override a Disabled key of the configuration:

```
launchctl enable gui/501/com.daemonology.veryfirstd
```

Note   Running bootstrap, you may see output like /Users/ alkenso/Desktop/com.daemonology.veryfirstd.plist: Service is disabled with a status of 119. This means the service has been disabled and needs to be enabled to be run.

The list command lists all the jobs loaded into launchd for the current user. Running it with sudo lists the system-wide daemons.

> **Note**   `list` is a legacy subcommand. But it is so simple and often used, so I mention it here.

The output has three columns: the PID of the job it is running, the last exit status of the job, and the job's label. If the exit status in this column is negative, it represents the negative of the signal that stopped the job. For example, "-15" indicates that the job has been exited with SIGTERM.

```
// List user agents for the current user
launchctl list

// List system daemons
sudo launchctl list
```

> **Note**   For these and more `launchctl` commands/subcommands, you may refer to man `launchctl(1)`. With the new macOS-ese, it has become more and more verbose and descriptive.

Additional and Informative Interface

This dumps the service's definition, properties, and metadata:

```
print <service-target>
```

Here's an example:

```
launchctl print gui/501/com.daemonology.veryfirstd
```

This prints the domain's metadata, including but not limited to all services in the domain.

```
print <domain-target>
```

Here's an example:

```
launchctl print system
launchctl print gui/501
```

This forces a service to start:

```
kickstart <service-target>
```

-k will kill and then restart existing instances.

```
launchctl kickstart gui/501/com.daemonology.veryfirstd
```

This sends a signal to a service's process:

```
kill <signame | signum> <service-target>
```

This sends a SIGTERM signal to the user agent of the user with a UID of 501:

```
launchctl kill TERM gui/501/com.daemonology.veryfirstd
```

If the service is running, the following prints a human-readable string describing why launchd launched the service. Note that this subcommand will show only the most appropriate reason.

```
blame <service-target>
```

launchctl Status Codes

The launchctl command status codes may be converted to strings using the xpc_strerror private function. For most status codes, launchctl uses an strerror function, but codes in the range [..] are treated separately.

You can find a full list of launchctl-specific statuses and their meaning in Chapter X.

The errors describe what launchctl error <code> is doing under the hood.

Legacy Interface (Before OS X 10.10)

The legacy interface is still working, but it's marked as deprecated by Apple.

The following loads the specified configuration files or directories of configuration files:

```
load | unload [-wF] paths ...
```

This is a predecessor of bootstrap | bootout.

If run as a user, it registers a user agent; if run as a root, it registers the system daemon.

It is usually used with both -wF flags.

- – -w: Enables/disables the job respectively for load/unload

- – -F: Forces the job to be registered/unregistered from the configuration.

This is a simple way of submitting a program to run without a configuration file:

```
submit -l <label> -- <command> [arg0] [arg1] [...]
```

This is about the same as registering a job with a plist:

```
<plist version="1.0">
<dict>
    <key>Label</key>
    <string><label></string>
    <key>ProgramArguments</key>
        <array>
            <string><command></string>
            <string><arg0></string>
            <string><arg1></string>
```

```
        </array>
    <key>KeepAlive</key>
    <true/>
</dict>
</plist>
```

This removes the job from `launchd` with a label. This subcommand will return immediately and not block until the job has been stopped.

`remove label`

This executes a given `<command>` as a user with `<UID>`:

asuser UID `command` **[args]**

It may be useful, for example, to load the job as a specific user from the root context.

Manage Daemons Programmatically

Apple provides a narrow public API that allows you to register daemons and agents.

It is limited to only a few daemons: privileged helpers (`//:ref`), login items (`//:ref`), and system extensions (`//:ref`). These APIs are discussed in detail in the corresponding chapters later in the book.

Real-world developers usually need access to the full power and flexibility of managing daemons and user agents. This chapter proposes two approaches to doing so.

launchctl + NSTask/Process

Unfortunately, Apple does not provide enough APIs to manage daemons and user agents programmatically.

But, we have a fully functional `launchctl` tool to manage them from the Terminal.

To fill this gap and maintain daemons and user agents from the app, I've created a library written in Swift that mirrors the `launchctl` tool.

The library is a wrapper around `launchctl` with handy interfaces.

It is available on GitHub and supports SPM integration (`https://github.com/Alkenso/sLaunchctl`).

The following are some examples of the `sLaunchctl` library usage. You can find the full abilities in the in-code library documentation.

Bootstrap
```
try launchctl.system.bootstrap(URL(fileURLWithPath: "/path/to/
com.my.daemon.plist"))
try launchctl.gui().bootstrap(URL(fileURLWithPath: "/path/to/
com.my.user_agent.plist"))
```

Bootout daemon
```
try launchctl.system.bootout(URL(fileURLWithPath: "/path/to/
com.my.daemon.plist"))
try launchctl.gui().bootout(URL(fileURLWithPath: "/path/to/com.
my.user_agent.plist"))
```

List all daemons
```
let rootDaemons = try launchctl.system.list()
let user505Agents = try launchctl.gui(505).list()
```

Also, the library supports the following (at the current moment):

- Bootstrap

- Bootout

- Enable/disable

- Listing daemons/agents

- Printing plain information about the domain target

- Printing plain information about the service target

- System, GUI, PID, user domain targets

jlaunchctl

Like the author says, "Force opensourced launchctl."

By applying reverse engineering techniques, some interface functions of launchd were revealed.

Based on low-level XPC routines, it is possible to communicate with launchd directly from the code to manage the daemons.

You can find detailed descriptions and sources at http://newosxbook. com/articles/jlaunchctl.html.

Although it's not quite as useful in production, jlaunchctl can be used, for example, in the following scenarios:

- To see how launchd communicates with another processes

- To reveal low-level XPC communication

- To manage launchd jobs when the launchctl tool is not available (a jailbroken iOS, for instance)

Warning   This method uses Apple's private API. Such an approach is quite unstable and is not guaranteed to be workable on new or updated versions of macOS.

---

launchd and launchctl Reference

Here are some useful references.

Useful Links and Manuals

Here are some materials related to daemon management through launchctl within launchd:

- https://ss64.com/osx/launchctl.html: Probably the best manual related to the launchctl command

- https://www.launchd.info/: Very informative reference of launchd job configuration plist keys

- man launchd.plist, man launchctl: Man pages related to job configuration and launchctl usage

Popular and Specific launchctl Errors

Here are a couple of common errors.

launchctl Typical Problems

Problem: launchctl returns "36: Operation is in progress" when bootstrap/bootout is invoked.

Solution: Just treat error 36 as OK. All scenarios where I've seen this were successful even when 36 error returned. If something went wrong, another error is displayed.

launchctl xpc_strerr Specific (Private) Errors

Listing 3-3 shows specific status codes.

Note   All errors below 107 can be printed in a human-readable form using strerror().

Listing 3-3. *launchctl Status Codes*

107: Malformed bundle
108: Invalid path
109: Invalid property list
110: Invalid or missing service identifier
111: Invalid or missing Program/ProgramArguments
112: Could not find specified domain
113: Could not find specified service
114: The specified username does not exist
115: The specified group does not exist
116: Routine not yet implemented
117: (n/a)
118: Bad response from server
119: Service is disabled
120: Bad subsystem destination for request
121: Path not searched for services
122: Path had bad ownership/permissions
123: Path is whitelisted for domain
124: Domain is tearing down
125: Domain does not support specified action
126: Request type is no longer supported
127: The specified service did not ship with the operating
      system
128: The specified path is not a bundle
129: The service was superseded by a later later version
130: The system encountered a condition where behavior was
      undefined
131: Out of order requests
132: Request for stale data
133: Multiple errors were returned; see stderr
134: Service cannot load in requested session

135: Process is not managed

136: Action not allowed on singleton service

137: Service does not support the specified action

138: Service cannot be loaded on this hardware

139: Service cannot presently execute

140: Service name is reserved or invalid

141: Reentrancy avoided

142: Operation only supported on development

143: Requested entry was cached

144: Requestor lacks required entitlement

145: Endpoint is hidden

146: Domain is in on-demand-only mode

147: The specified service did not ship in the requestor

148: The specified service path was not in the service cache

149: Could not find a bundle of the given identifier through LaunchServices

150: Operation not permitted while System Integrity Protection is engaged

151: A complete hack

152: Service cannot load in current boot environment

153: Completely unexpected error

154: Requestor is not a platform binary

155: Refusing to execute/trust quarantined program/file

156: Domain creation with that UID is not allowed anymore

157: System service is not in system service whitelist

158: Service cannot be loaded on current os variant

159: Unknown error

PART II

Daemons in Detail

CHAPTER 4

Daemons at a Glance

Generally, there are only two main types of daemons: daemons (root) and user agents (user).

For convenience, in the following chapters, we will use Apple's terminology and classification of the daemons. This classification considers specifics of installation, registration, permissions, and restrictions of the daemons when categorizing them.

We will cover the following terms (all of them are daemons/user agents):

- Daemons

- User agents

- Privileged helpers

- Login items

- XPC service

- System extensions

Figure 4-1 shows how to choose the best daemon type for your needs.

© Volodymyr Vashurkin 2021
V. Vashurkin, *macOS Daemonology*, https://doi.org/10.1007/978-1-4842-7277-0_4

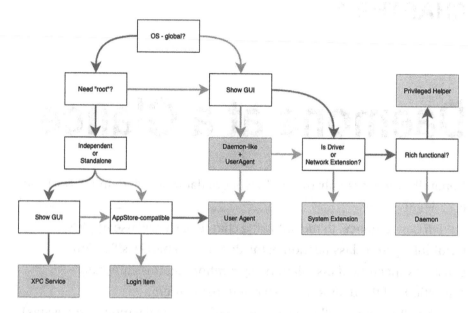

Figure 4-1. *Considerations when choosing the right daemon type*

XPC Overview

In macOS, daemons usually are tightly bound to the native interprocess communication mechanism: the XPC.

XPC is designed in classic terms of a client-server architecture.

Connections are clients, and a listener is a server.

XPC communication is a big and complex topic. It is discussed in Part III of this book.

CHAPTER 5

Classic Daemon

This chapter covers the specifics of "classic" daemons such as root background processes.

As mentioned in previous chapters, we decided to use the term *daemon* to classify the exact kind of launchd service: system-wide daemons that are not privilege helpers or system extensions.

Daemon Specifics

Daemons are:

- System-wide

- Run as root

- Usually the single instance in the system

- Stand-alone and independent

- Any executable (command-line, bundle, or script)

Naming Conventions

Daemons in macOS have their own naming convention:

- Lowercase

- Letter *d* at the end

- Examples: `installd`, `akd`, `launchd`, `rapportd`, `replayd`, `powerd`

© Volodymyr Vashurkin 2021
V. Vashurkin, *macOS Daemonology*, https://doi.org/10.1007/978-1-4842-7277-0_5

When to Use

Consider using daemons for the following:

- To perform operations as a root

- When the daemon is your main app or stand-alone component

- To synchronize the work of multiple per-user apps

- To interact with KEXT

Here are some examples:

- Antivirus monitoring and scanning

- Shared control center of multi-user app

- Filesystem server (SSH, FTP, and so on)

- IRC/messaging

Install and Register

Daemons usually are installed and registered in the system in a few different ways.

- If the `.plist` file is placed in `/Library/LaunchDaemons`, the daemon bootstraps automatically on system startup.

- Bootstrapped with the `launchctl` tool from any location.

To install the daemon, you need the following:

1. Prepare the `launchd` daemon's plist file (as described at `<link>`).

2. Prepare the tool/script you want to be run as the daemon.

3. [optional] Place the `.plist` file at `/Library/LaunchDaemons` to be sure your daemon will be bootstrapped each time the system boots.

4. [optional] Run the `launchctl` bootstrap as described at `<link>` to immediately bootstrap your daemon's `sudo launchctl` bootstrap system. `/path/to/com.daemonology.testd.plist`

XPC Communication

To communicate via XPC, the daemon's plist should contain Mach services related to the daemon.

Here's an example:

```
<key><MachServices></key>
<dict>
        <key>com.daemonology.testd.xpc</key>
        </true>
</dict>
```

// Client side
```
// ObjC
[[NSXPCConnection alloc] initWithMachServiceName: @"com.daemonology.testd.xpc" options: NSXPCConnectionPrivileged]
```

```
// Swift
NSXPCConnection(machServiceName: "com.daemonology.testd.xpc",
options: .privileged)
```

// Daemon side

```
// ObjC
[[NSXPCListener alloc] initWithMachServiceName:
@"com.daemonology.testd.xpc"]
```

```
// Swift
NSXPCListener(machServiceName: "com.daemonology.testd.xpc")
```

Known Restrictions or Limitations

The .plist configuration file must have 700..755 permissions.

CHAPTER 6

Privileged Helper

In this chapter, we'll discuss special daemons, called *privileged helpers*, which are the legal and modern way to do privilege escalation in macOS.

You can also refer to the examples at Daemonology/3-PrivilegedHelper.

PrivilegedHelper Specifics

PrivilegedHelper looks very much like the regular daemon with the following attributes:

- System-wide

- Run as root

- Usually a single instance in the system

But PrivilegedHelper has some differences and limitations.

- It is installed and managed by a limited list of apps (declared in Info.plist).

- Only command-line tools are supported.

Generally, PrivilegeHelper is an almost the only legal and simple way of performing privilege escalation and performing root actions. A special case is SystemExtension, but we'll speak about that later (in Chapter 7).

© Volodymyr Vashurkin 2021
V. Vashurkin, *macOS Daemonology*, https://doi.org/10.1007/978-1-4842-7277-0_6

> **Note**   There is also the `AuthorizationExecuteWithPrivileges`
> function for privileged code execution, but it has been deprecated since
> OS X 10.7, it leads to vulnerabilities and security breaches, and it may
> not work in future macOS systems.

Naming Conventions

Privileged helpers in macOS have their own naming conventions.

- Reverse domain name notation

- Capital letters and dots allowed

- The word `Helper` at the end preferred

- Examples: `AirPlayXPCHelper`, `com.apple.AccountPolicyHelper`,
  `com.apple.CodeSigningHelper`, `com.developer.ProxyHelper`

When to Use

Consider using `PrivilegedHelper` in the following cases:

- When performing one-time root operations

- When performing simple root operations

Here are some examples:

- Installers and uninstallers that need root privileges

- Copying/removing files as root

- Registering/unregistering root daemons

- Loading/unloading KEXTs

Install and Register

Here I'll provide a step-by-step guide to creating, setting up, registering, and communicating with the `PrivilegeHelper` tool.

The following is the overall process:

1. Create an app (or use an existing one).

2. Create a `PrivilegedHelper` command-line tool.

3. Create a `PrivilegedHelper` `launchd.plist`.

4. Codesign requirements.

5. SMJobBless.

6. XPC communication.

As an example, we will create a simple GUI application that uses `PrivilegeHelper` to write a startup log string into a file at a location that can be modified only with root privileges: `/Library/Application Support/Daemonology.log`.

Step 1: Create the App (or Use an Existing One)

Just create a typical GUI application. The language of the app does not matter, but for consistency we will go with Swift. See Figure 6-1.

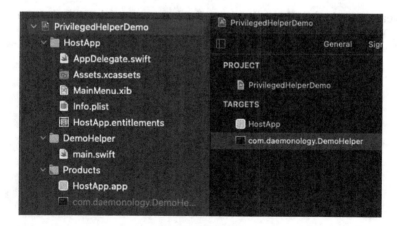

Figure 6-1. *Host application target*

Step 2: Create a PrivilegedHelper Command-Line Tool

Create a command-line tool called DemoHelper. It will act like a privileged helper for our example.

Apple recommends setting a name for the PrivilegeHelper equivalent to its BundleIdentifier, so we will follow this rule and call our helper com.daemonology.DemoHelper. See Figure 6-2.

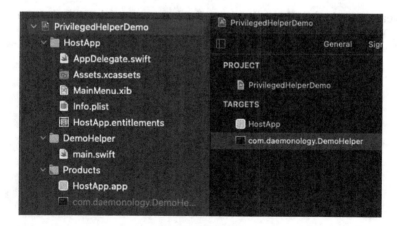

Figure 6-2. *Privileged helper target*

The important thing that our helper is missing is the Info.plist file.

By default, command-line tools are created without such a file, so let's fix that by adding a typical Info.plist file with simple content, as shown in Listing 6-1.

Listing 6-1. PrivilegeHelper Info.plist

```
<plist version="1.0">
<dict>
        <key>CFBundleIdentifier</key>
        <string>$(PRODUCT_BUNDLE_IDENTIFIER)</string>
        <key>CFBundleInfoDictionaryVersion</key>
        <string>6.0</string>
        <key>CFBundleShortVersionString</key>
        <string>1.0</string>
        <key>CFBundleVersion</key>
        <string>0</string>
</dict>
</plist>
```

Also, specify the file Info.plist in the DemoHelper build settings by following these steps:

1. Embed Info.plist into the binary as an additional section. This is required by later API checks.

2. Set the path to the Info.plist file.

3. Make sure the bundle identifier is set and equals the helper's product name. See Figure 6-3.

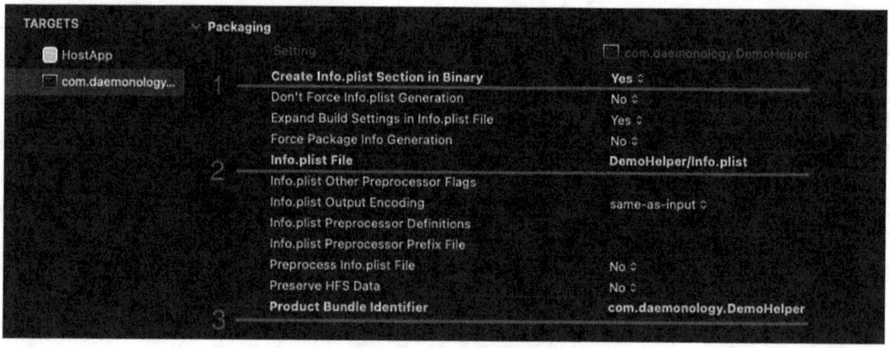

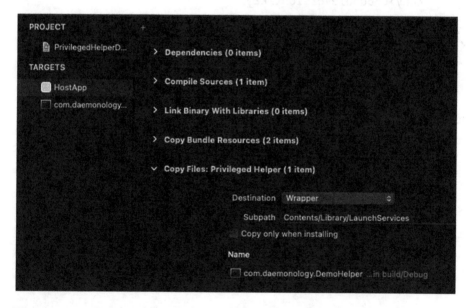

Figure 6-3. *Privilege helper build settings*

Finally, copy DemoHelper into a specific place in the HostApp bundle.
According to Apple, privileged helpers should be placed inside the
main app bundle at the relative path Contents/Library/LaunchServices.
See Figure 6-4.

Figure 6-4. *Copying the privilege helper to the host application*

Step 3: PrivilegedHelper launchd.plist

The created tool is designed to be a PrivilegeHelper. PrivilegeHelper is a sort of daemons. And every daemon needs a launchd configuration plist.

As for PrivilegeHelper, we must provide this configuration ourselves.

First, create the launchd.plist file with our helper launchd configuration (the simplest way to do this). See Listing 6-2.

Listing 6-2. Privilege Helper launchd Configuration Plist

```
<plist version="1.0">
<dict>
     <key>Label</key>
     <string>com.daemonology.demohelper</string>
     <key>MachServices</key>
     <dict>
          <key>com.daemonology.demohelper.logger.xpc</key>
          <true/>
     </dict>
</dict>
</plist>
```

As you can see, this configuration is not full. At a minimum, it lacks the Program/Program Arguments key. That is because the system itself will determine where to put the executable during the helper installation process.

Place the launchd.plist file near the rest of the DemoHelper source code.

Now, let's add a bit of magic to make things work.

To make the PrivilegedHelper installation API happy, we should embed this configuration into the binary in an additional section.

It is made by extending Other Linker Flags setting with the following, as shown in Figure 6-5:

```
OTHER_LDFLAGS = -sectcreate __TEXT __launchd_plist DemoHelper/
launchd.plist
```

Figure 6-5. *Embedding launchd.plist into the privilege helper binary*

Step 4: Codesign Requirements

Apple takes care of safety and security. Therefore, privileged helpers can be managed by only predefined applications. To make such checks, Apple uses codesign information.

What does that mean for us?

For both HostApp and DemoHelper, we must specify information about another one using the corresponding Info.plist file as well as provide specific codesign requirements.

If and only if the tool is in the list and the requirements are met will the PrivilegeHelper installation API succeed.

Add the SMAuthorizedClients array into DemoHelper's Info.plist file. See Figure 6-6.

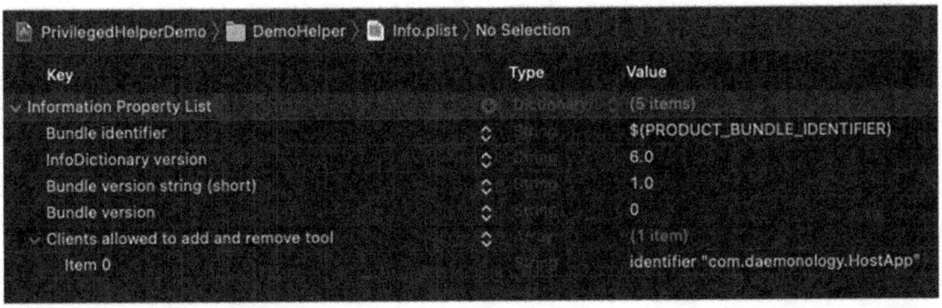

Figure 6-6. *SMJobBless codesign requirements, PrivilegedHelper side*

Add the SMPrivilegedExecutables dict into HostApp's Info.plist. See Figure 6-7.

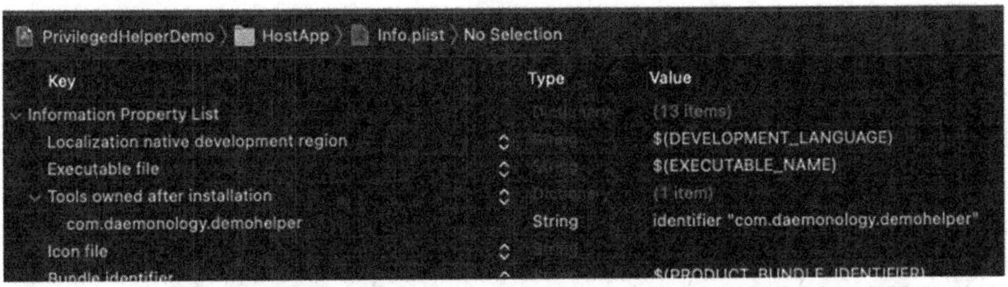

Figure 6-7. *SMJobBless codesign requirements, host application side*

A Bit More About Codesign Requirements

For development, there are enough codesign requirements with a bundle identifier only (as shown earlier).

For production, it is unsafe and should be extended. Practice shows that good and simple requirements can be extended with one of the following:

- Certificate author (subject.CN). Here's an example:

  ```
  anchor apple generic and certificate leaf[subject.
  CN] = "Apple Development: macdeveloper@
  mail.com (Z22M55HV7V)" and certificate 1[fie
  ld.1.2.840.113635.100.6.2.1] /* exists */
  ```

- Personal development team (subject.OU). This usually
  works for debug builds. Here's an example:

  ```
  anchor apple generic and certificate 1[fie
  ld.1.2.840.113635.100.6.2.1] /* exists */ and
  certificate leaf[subject.OU] = "$(DEVELOPMENT_
  TEAM)"
  ```

- Development team (subject.OU). This usually works
  for release builds with a Developer ID Application
  signature. Here's an example:

  ```
  anchor apple generic and (certificate leaf
  [field.1.2.840.113635.100.6.1.9] /* exists */ or
  certificate 1[field.1.2.840.113635.100.6.2.6]
  /* exists */ and certificate leaf[fie
  ld.1.2.840.113635.100.6.1.13] /* exists */ and
  certificate leaf[subject.OU] = "$(DEVELOPMENT_
  TEAM)")
  ```

You can read more about the requirements language in the
official documentation: https://developer.apple.com/library/
archive/documentation/Security/Conceptual/CodeSigningGuide/
RequirementLang/RequirementLang.html.

Step 5: SMJobBless

Finally, we are ready to install our helper into the system.

To install the PrivilegeHelper, Apple has ServiceManagement.
framework with a single nondeprecated function: SMJobBless.

As a precondition, SMJobBless requires the authorization right called
kSMRightBlessPrivilegedHelper.

AuthorizationRef with this right can be acquired using the Authorization API and usually leads to administrator password prompting. See Listing 6-3.

Listing 6-3. SMJobBless

```swift
// wrap the function in Swift
func blessHelper(label: String, auth: AuthorizationRef) -> Bool
{
    var error: Unmanaged<CFError>?
    let blessStatus = SMJobBless(kSMDomainSystemLaunchd, label
    as CFString, auth, &error)

    if !blessStatus {
        NSLog("[SMJBS]: Helper bless failed with error \
        (error!.takeUnretainedValue())")
    }

    return blessStatus
}

// and call it for our helper
blessHelper(label: "com.daemonology.demohelper", auth: authRef)
```

What does SMJobBless actually do under the hood? Here's a list:

- Copy the helper binary into a safe location and set root permissions

- Verify the codesign of the copied helper and check if the requirements match

- Move the copied and verified helper into /Library/ PrivilegedHelperTools (may change in future macOS versions)

– Read launchd.plist from the binary section and create a valid daemon plist at /Library/LaunchDaemons

– Bootstrap the helper as a system daemon

Troubleshooting

If you create PrivilegedHelper from scratch and successfully run SMJobBless, you are lucky!

SMJobBless can fail for one of the reasons. See Listing 6-4.

Listing 6-4. SMJobBless Error Codes

```
* @const kSMErrorInternalFailure
* An internal failure has occurred.
*
* @const kSMErrorInvalidSignature
* The Application's code signature does not meet the
requirements to perform
* the operation.
*
* @const kSMErrorAuthorizationFailure
* The request required authorization (i.e. adding a job to the
* {@link kSMDomainSystemLaunchd} domain) but the
AuthorizationRef did not
* contain the required right.
*
* @const kSMErrorToolNotValid
* The specified path does not exist or the tool at the
specified path is not
* valid.
*
* @const kSMErrorJobNotFound
```

```
* A job with the given label could not be found.
*
* @const kSMErrorServiceUnavailable
* The service required to perform this operation is unavailable
or is no longer
* accepting requests.
*/
enum {
      kSMErrorInternalFailure = 2,
      kSMErrorInvalidSignature,
      kSMErrorAuthorizationFailure,
      kSMErrorToolNotValid,
      kSMErrorJobNotFound,
      kSMErrorServiceUnavailable,
      kSMErrorJobPlistNotFound,
      kSMErrorJobMustBeEnabled,
      kSMErrorInvalidPlist,
};
```

This documentation is great, but sometimes it is not enough. Here is additional meaning of some errors.

The following indicates a general issue. For example, the helper tool plists are wrong, the filename is incorrect, or the file is in the wrong location.

`kSMErrorInternalFailure (2)`

The following indicates that the tool cannot be found at all (for example, the helper tool is not in `project1.app/Contents/Library/LaunchServices/`):

`kSMErrorToolNotValid (5)`

The following indicates invalid `SMAuthorizedClients/SMPrivilegedE` `xecutables` sections in `Info.plist`:

```
kSMErrorAuthorizationFailure = 4
```

Here are the steps to xx:

1. Be careful with quotes. Sometimes quotes turn into smart quotes, which is another symbol. The symbols ' " ' must be ' `&quot;` ' in the raw plist representation. See Figure 6-8.

```
<key>CFBundleVersion</key>
<string>0</string>
<key>SMAuthorizedClients</key>
<array>
    <string>identifier &quot;com.daemonology.HostApp&quot;</string>
</array>
</dict>
</plist>
```

Figure 6-8. *Invalid quotes in Info.plist file*

2. Invalid codesign requirements. Find errors using the `SMJobBlessUtil.py` script.

For troubleshooting, Apple provides a special `SMJobBlessUtil.py` script at `https://developer.apple.com/library/archive/samplecode/` `SMJobBless/Listings/SMJobBlessUtil_py.html`.

To check if everything looks fine, use this:

```
SMJobBlessUtil.py check  /path/to/build_products/app
```

To set the correct requirements, use this:

```
SMJobBlessUtil.py setreq /path/to/build_products/app /path/to/
app/Info.plist /path/to/tool/Info.plist
```

Step 6: XPC Communication

Communicating with `PrivilegedHelper` is the same as with a regular daemon.

On the app side, we create an `XPCConnection` with `machServiceName` plus privileged options.

On the helper side, `XPCListener` with `machServiceName`.

The `HostApp` code looks like Listing 6-5.

Listing 6-5. Host Application Side

```
func applicationDidFinishLaunching(_ aNotification:
Notification) {
    // When the host starts, perform
    // - get AuthorizationRef asking the user for it
    // - install the privilege helper (bless helper via SMJobBless)
    // - create XPC connection to the helper
    // - perform privileged action by helper via XPC connection

        guard let authorization = askAuthorization() else {
        showMessage("Failed to get authorization.")
        return
    }

    guard blessHelper(label: kPrivilegedHelperLabel,
    authorization: authorization) else {
        showMessage("Failed to bless \(kPrivilegedHelperLabel).")
        return
    }

    let connection = NSXPCConnection(machServiceName:
    kPrivilegedHelperMachName, options: .privileged)
    connection.remoteObjectInterface = NSXPCInterface(with:
    DAEPrivilegedOperations.self)

    connection.resume()
```

```
let remoteProxy = connection.
remoteObjectProxyWithErrorHandler { (error) in
    DispatchQueue.main.async { NSAlert(error: error).
    runModal() }
}

guard let privilegedOps = remoteProxy as?
DAEPrivilegedOperations else {
    showMessage("Invalid connection setup.")
    return
}

let package = URL(fileURLWithPath: "/path/to/package.pkg"
privilegedOps.installPackage(package)) { installed in
    DispatchQueue.main.async {
        showMessage("Helper installed the package = \
        (installed)")
    }
}
}
```

The DemoHelper side is also simple; see Listing 6-6.

Listing 6-6. PrivilegedHelper Side

```
// Auxiliary class that handles:
// - incoming XPC connections
// - DAEPrivilegedOperations calls over XPC
class Helper: NSObject { }

extension Helper: DAEPrivilegedOperations {
    func installPackage(_ package: URL, completion:
    DAEInstallPackageCompletion) {
        NSLog("Installing the package \(package)")
```

```
            completion(true)
    }
}

extension Helper: NSXPCListenerDelegate {
    func listener(_ listener: NSXPCListener,
    shouldAcceptNewConnection newConnection: NSXPCConnection)
    -> Bool {
        newConnection.exportedInterface = NSXPCInterface(with:
        DAEPrivilegedOperations.self)
        newConnection.exportedObject = self
        newConnection.resume()
        return true
    }
}

let helper = Helper()
let listener = NSXPCListener(machServiceName:
kPrivilegedHelperMachName)
listener.delegate = helper
listener.resume()

RunLoop.main.run()
```

PrivilegeHelper: Developers' Guide

intro text:

1. Create the app (or use an existing one) and a
    command-line tool for `PrivilegedHelper`.

    –   Name `PrivilegedHelper` the same as its bundle identifier.

    –   Copy the helper into the app's wrapper at
        `Contents/Library/LaunchServices`.

2. Do the following for the `PrivilegedHelper Info.plist` file:

   – Add `Info.plist` for the helper.

   – Add an option to embed it into the binary.

3. Do the following for the `PrivilegedHelper launchd.plist` file:

   – Add `launchd.plist` with the `PrivilegedHelper launchd` service specifics.

   – Set `Label` equal to the helper's bundle identifier.

   – Add one or multiple XPC endpoints into the `MachServices` dictionary. The key is `com.company.endpoint.name.xpc, Value = YES`.

   – Embed `launchd.plist` into the helper's binary in a custom section via Other Linker Flags.

4. Here are the codesign requirements:

   – Add the requirements with the `SMAuthorizedClients` array into the helper's `Info.plist`. Item = requirements.

   – Add the requirements with the `SMPrivilegedExecutables` dict into the app's `Info.plist`. The key is the helper's bundle identifier. value = requirements.

   – Ensure the quotes are normal ones, not "smart."

5. SMJobBless:

    −   Import the ServiceManagement framework.

    −   Create AuthorizationRef with the right
        kSMRightBlessPrivilegedHelper.

    −   Perform troubleshooting with SMJobBlessUtil.py.

6. XPC commuication:

    −   Use MachServiceName in the same way as one of
        MachServices in launchd.plist.

    −   The app (client side) creates a connection with
        machServiceName and the privileged option.

    −   The helper (listener side) creates a listener with
        machServiceName.

    −   Secure your XPC connection (see Chapter 15).

Known Restrictions and Limitations of Frameworks and Shared Libraries

When SMJobBless succeeds, PrivilegedHelper is registered in launchd, but the binary to launch now is copied to /Library/LaunchDaemons.

This leads to some restrictions because PrivilegedHelper cannot be a bundled daemon (i.e., have resources).

PrivilegedHelper should not be linked against custom dynamic libraries or frameworks.

Because the binary is copied, usually it cannot find the necessary frameworks to link against. There are possible workarounds such as placing custom frameworks or resources at a persistent path and telling PrivilegeHelper how to find them.

For example, you can place your shared resources/frameworks here:

- /Library/Frameworks or /Library/Application
  Support/com.company.Company/...

- /Applications/YourApp.app/Contents/...

Be careful: changing the placement of such shared resources will lead to PrivilegeHelper being unstable or crashing.

Using Swift in PrivilegedHelper

In the documentation, Apple says not to write PrivilegedHelperTools in Swift. This is because the Swift standard libraries have shipped with macOS only since macOS 10.14 Catalina. One possible workaround for this is to install the Swift Runtime Support package before accessing your PrivilegedHelper.

CHAPTER 7

System Extensions (Since macOS 10.15)

This chapter gives an overview of a new daemon type called *system extensions* (SEXTs) that have been available since macOS 10.15 Catalina.

You can see examples at `Daemonology/4-SystemExtension`.

System extensions extend the functionality of macOS without requiring kernel-level access. Therefore, SEXTs are positioned as modern, safe, and secure replacements for kernel extensions (KEXTs).

At the moment, system extensions are intended for the following:

- Security solutions

- Network extensions

- DriverKit device drivers (a replacement for IOKit)

What is a SEXT from a daemonology perspective?

A SEXT is a mix of a classic daemon and a privilege helper, gaining mostly conveniences from the two rather than any limitations.

© Volodymyr Vashurkin 2021
V. Vashurkin, *macOS Daemonology*, https://doi.org/10.1007/978-1-4842-7277-0_7

System Extensions Specifics

System extensions have the following attributes:

- System-wide

- Run as root

- Usually a single instance in the system

- Installed and managed by concrete applications

- Always bundled

- Must be placed inside parent application bundle

- Parent application must be placed into the /Applications folder

- In some cases allowed for AppStore

Naming Conventions

System extensions in macOS have their own naming conventions.

- Reverse domain name notation

- Has suffix .systemextension

- Capital letters and dots allowed

- Prefer to include name of the main app

- Example:
  com.daemonology.HostApp.SEXTDemo.systemextension

When to Use

Consider using SEXTs in the following instances:

— To implement a device driver (using DriverKit)

— To use EndpointSecurity

— To implement a network extension

— To replace legacy KEXT functionality

Here are some examples:

— Antiviruses, data leak prevention/protection (DLP), advanced administration, and so on

— Network filters, VPN, and so on

— Custom USB device driver

In order to work, a system extension must be one of the following:

— DEXT (a DriverKit driver)

— NetworkExtension (with entitlement com.apple. developer.networking.networkextension)

— EndpointSecurity (with entitlement com.apple. developer.endpoint-security.client)

If none of these is true, the system extension will not be loaded.

Important note   In most Apple's articles, SEXTs are positioned as a good place to implement functionality for security solutions, including a new EndpointSecurity framework.

Probably, in future releases of macOS, a SEXT will be the only place where the ES framework works. But for now (macOS BigSur), the ES framework also nicely works within any root process, including regular daemons.

Usage Specifics

Here are some specifics about SEXTs:

- Once the SEXT is loaded, the user must approve the SEXT installation in Security Preferences.

- Once the SEXT is unloaded, the corresponding authorization is needed. Usually users are prompted for an admin password.

- Once the application is moved to the trash or deleted, the system automatically notifies about installing the SEXT and unloading and deleting it.

Install and Register

Here is how to install and register a SEXT.

Step 1: Create the App (or Use an Existing One)

Just create a regular GUI application called HostApp. The language of the app does not matter, but for consistency I will go with Swift.

For the HostApp application, do the following:

1. Add the entitlement com.apple.developer.system-extension.install.

2. Enable the hardened runtime.

Step 2: Create a System Extension

For some reason, Xcode (currently 12.5) does not provide any templates for a pure system extension.

The most appropriate way is to create and change the NetworkExtension target. See Figure 7-1.

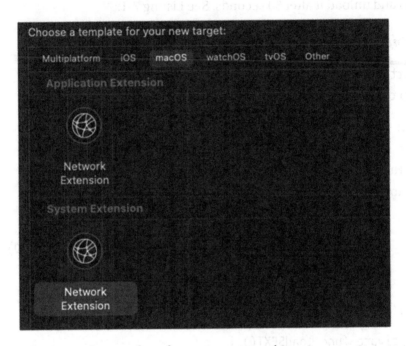

Figure 7-1. *Xcode template for system extensions*

When created, remove all the NetworkExtension-specific code.

– Remove all the .swift files, leaving only main.swift.

– Remove the NetworkExtension key from Info.plist.

– Remove the NetworkExtension-related entitlements.

Step 3: Loading and Unloading

SystemExtension.framework provides a simple and obvious interface for managing system extensions.

It supports two request types: load and unload.

For example purposes, I'm going to load a SEXT when the application starts and unload it after 30 seconds. See Listing 7-1.

Listing 7-1. System Extensions Load/Unload Routines

```
import Cocoa
import SystemExtensions

@main
class AppDelegate: NSObject, NSApplicationDelegate {
    func applicationDidFinishLaunching(_ aNotification:
    Notification) {
        loadSEXT()

        DispatchQueue.main.asyncAfter(deadline: .now() + 30) {
            self.unloadSEXT()
        }
    }

    private func loadSEXT() {
        let request = OSSystemExtensionRequest.
        activationRequest(
            forExtensionWithIdentifier: "com.daemonology.
            HostApp.SEXTDemo",
            queue: .global()
        )
        request.delegate = self
        OSSystemExtensionManager.shared.submitRequest(request)
    }
```

```
private func unloadSEXT() {
    let request = OSSystemExtensionRequest.
    deactivationRequest(
        forExtensionWithIdentifier: "com.daemonology.
        HostApp.SEXTDemo",
        queue: .global()
    )
    request.delegate = self
    OSSystemExtensionManager.shared.submitRequest(request)
}
}
```

Note   The SystemExtension installation (activation) mechanism is pretty similar to PrivilegedHelper's SMJobBless.

Under the hood, the activation request does the following:

- Checks the codesign requirements of both HostApp and the SEXT

- Checks if HostApp is placed correctly (into the / Applications folder)

- Copies a SEXT into a specific system location

- Registers a SEXT within launchd

The deactivation request, on its turn, also has a complex job, doing the following:

- Terminates the SEXT process.

- Unloads the SEXT from launchd.

- Marks the SEXT as inactive. This means that the SEXT will be deleted only after system reboot.

The SystemExtension request API needs a delegate that conforms to the protocol OSSystemExtensionRequestDelegate that is asked/notified about. See Listing 7-2.

- SEXT requests user for approval

- SEXT did load

- SEXT load did fail

- Behavior of upgrading existing SEXT versus new one

Listing 7-2. System Extensions Load/Unload Delegate Methods

```swift
extension AppDelegate: OSSystemExtensionRequestDelegate {
    func request(
        _ request: OSSystemExtensionRequest,
        actionForReplacingExtension existing:
        OSSystemExtensionProperties,
        withExtension ext: OSSystemExtensionProperties
    ) -> OSSystemExtensionRequest.ReplacementAction {
        print(#function)
        return .replace
    }

    func requestNeedsUserApproval(
        _ request: OSSystemExtensionRequest
    ) {
        print(#function)
    }

    func request(
        _ request: OSSystemExtensionRequest,
        didFinishWithResult result: OSSystemExtensionRequest.
        Result
```

```
) {
    print(#function)
}

func request(
    _ request: OSSystemExtensionRequest,
    didFailWithError error: Error
) {
    print("\(#function): \(error)")
}
}
```

When a SEXT is going to be loaded (via OSSystemExtensionRequest.
activationRequest), macOS prompts the user for approval. In Security
Preferences, the user should manually allow the system extension to be loaded.

macOS does not cache the user resolution. So, if the extension has
been unloaded and is loaded a second time, the prompt will appear again.
See Figure 7-2.

Figure 7-2. *System extension installation process*

Figure 7-2. (*continued*)

Invocation of OSSystemExtensionRequest.deactivationRequest causes the SEXT to be unloaded.

The unload action requires additional privileges. See Figure 7-3.

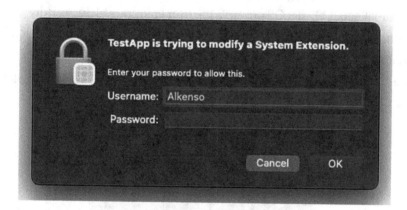

Figure 7-3. *System extension uninstallation process*

When the application containing the SEXT is going to be moved to the trash, it automatically triggers the deactivationRequest alert message, as shown in Figure 7-4.

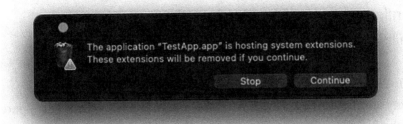

Figure 7-4. *System extension removal when application is moved to trash*

Step 4: Troubleshooting

The following are some troubleshooting tips:

- OSSystemExtensionError::validationFailed
  (code = 9): This checks if the hardened runtime is
  enabled for the app and SEXT. It also checks if the SEXT
  is a kind of DEXT or contains the necessary entitlements
  (described at the beginning of the chapter).

- OSSystemExtensionError::missingEntitlement
  (code = 2): This checks if the system extension
  entitlement is added to the HostApp.

XPC Communication

System extensions are designed in such a way that you can interact with them using XPC.

> **Warning** An exception is that DriverKit drivers (DEXTs) are communicated via the IOKit API.

Unlike daemons/privilege helpers, you are not allowed to specify a launchd configuration plist. SEXT's plist is generated and bootstrapped in launchd inside the SEXT management API.

As a user, you can communicate with the system extension via XPC as with the usual root daemon.

The XPC endpoint name is predefined, as shown in Listing 7-3.

Listing 7-3. SEXT XPC Communication

```
let sextMachServiceName = "\(TeamID).\(BundleID).xpc"

// HostApp side
let connection = NSXPCConnection(machServiceName:
sextMachServiceName, options: .privileged)

// SEXT side
let connection = NSXPCListener(machServiceName:
sextMachServiceName)
```

The rest of the XPC communication is standard.

Management Tool: systemextensionsctl

Similar to launchctl, Apple has released a SystemExtension-specific tool for managing SEXTs called systemextensionsctl.

Currently, here is the systemextensionsctl usage:

- systemextensionsctl developer [on|off]: Enables the ability to perform SEXT loading from any directory, not only from /Applications.

- `systemextensionsctl list [category]`: Lists all installed system extensions (both activated and deactivated).

- `systemextensionsctl reset`: Resets the state of all system extensions.

- `systemextensionsctl uninstall <teamId> <bundleId>`: Also accepts - for the team ID and performs `SystemExtension` deactivation from the Terminal.

For the debugging and Testing System Extensions, consider reading Apple's article at `https://developer.apple.com/documentation/driverkit/debugging_and_testing_system_extensions?language=objc`.

CHAPTER 8

User Agents

In this chapter, we'll discuss the specifics of user agents, which are user background processes.

User Agent Specifics

User agents have the following attributes:

- Run as a specific user
- Usually multiple instances in the system (a process for one user)
- Stand-alone and independent
- Any executable (command line, bundle, or script)

Naming Conventions

User agents in macOS have their own naming conventions.

- CapitalCamelCase
- The word `Agent` at the end
- Examples: `AirPlayUIAgent`, `AMPArtworkAgent`, `ContextStoreAgent`, `KernelEventAgent`

© Volodymyr Vashurkin 2021
V. Vashurkin, *macOS Daemonology*, https://doi.org/10.1007/978-1-4842-7277-0_8

When to Use

Lots of modern applications such as mail clients, notes, sharing tools, etc., have their own user agents. Often you can see the existing user agents of a particular application by looking at the menu bar.

Consider using user agents in the following cases:

- Background applications

- Main application helpers

- To synchronize work if an application is split into multiple processes

Here are some examples:

- MenuBar icon application

- Showing notifications even when the app is closed

- Limited version of the app without requiring administrator rights

- Showing the user a minimalistic UI for a system-wide daemon

- Implementing login hooks

Install and Register

User agents usually are installed and registered in the system in a few different ways.

- If the .plist file is placed in /Library/LaunchAgents, the agent bootstraps automatically on user login *for each user*.

- If the .plist file is placed in $HOME/Library/
  LaunchAgents, the agent bootstraps automatically on
  login only for *this user*.

- User agents are bootstrapped with the launchctl tool
  from any location.

To install the user agent, you need to do the following:

1. Prepare the user agent's launchd plist file
   (as described at <link>).

2. Prepare the tool/script you want to be run as the
   user agent.

3. [optional] Place the .plist file at /Library/
   LaunchAgents or $HOME/Library/LaunchAgents
   to be sure your user agent will be bootstrapped
   each time the user logs in.

4. [optional] Run launchctl bootstrap as described
   at <link> to immediately bootstrap your user agent
   as follows:

   launchctl bootstrap gui/501 /path/to/com.daemonology.
   UserAgentDemo.plist

XPC Communication

To communicate via XPC, a user agent's plist should contain Mach services
related to the user agent. Generally, it's the same story as with daemons.

Listing 8-1. UserAgent XPC Specifics

```
<key><MachServices></key>
<dict>
      <key>com.daemonology.testd.xpc</key>
      </true>
</dict>

// ObjC
[[NSXPCConnection alloc] initWithMachServiceName:
@"com.daemonology.UserAgent.xpc" options: 0]

// Swift
NSXPCConnection(machServiceName: "com.daemonology.UserAgent.xpc",
options: [])

Daemon should prepare XPC listener:
// ObjC
[[NSXPCListener alloc] initWithMachServiceName: @"com.
daemonology.UserAgent.xpc"]

// Swift
NSXPCListener(machServiceName: "com.daemonology.UserAgent.xpc")
```

User Agent Development Notes

Here are some important tidbits.

Background UI Application

Some applications are designed to be background apps initially.

They don't have icons in the Dock, but they still have a limited or full user interface with windows, dialogs, etc.

First, the Info.plist key to pay attention to is LSUIElement, which can help to achieve the desired behavior. The presence of this key tells the system that the application is an agent. Such applications will not appear in App Switch, the Force Quit window, and the Dock. You can find more information at https://developer.apple.com/library/archive/ documentation/General/Reference/InfoPlistKeyReference/Articles/ LaunchServicesKeys.html.

In some cases, the app needs to show an icon in the status bar, as shown in Figure 8-1.

Figure 8-1. *Status bar example*

For such functional classes, NSStatusBar, NSStatusItem, and NSStatusBarButton can be used.

This functional class is beyond the book's topic. You can find more information here:

- https://developer.apple.com/documentation/ appkit/nsstatusbar

- https://caseybrant.com/2019/02/20/macos-menu- bar-extras.html

CHAPTER 9

XPC Services

In this chapter, we'll discuss the simplest type of daemon: an XPC service.

XPCService is probably the simplest form of daemon in macOS from the developer's perspective. XPC services are usually lightweight helper tools that run and perform work on demand.

XPC Service Specifics

Here are some XPC service specifics:

- Tightly bound to a specific app

- Run as a user

- Always background; don't show a UI

- Bundled executable

- May be embedded into the framework

- AppStore compatible

Naming Conventions

An XPC service in macOS has its own naming conventions.

- Reverse domain name notation preferred

- Usually ends with Service

© Volodymyr Vashurkin 2021
V. Vashurkin, *macOS Daemonology*, https://doi.org/10.1007/978-1-4842-7277-0_9

- Capital letters and dots allowed

- May include the name of the main app

- Examples:

```
com.apple.dt.Xcode.DeveloperSystemPolicyService,
VTEncoderXPCService
```

When to Use

Using XPC services allows you to split the app into logically separated modules. Such functionality will not even be loaded into memory unless the main app requests it. For example, there are some costly but infrequent tasks such as encoding, encryption, compression, and so on.

Breaking applications into XPC services can help to keep the main application simpler and take less memory while running, running only our XPC service on demand.

One way or another, XPC services are a kind of a daemon. An XPC service still runs as a separate process. If that process crashes or it's killed, it doesn't affect the main application. For example, if you are going to use some unstable code or user-provided plugin-based approach, XPC services may come to the rescue. If an XPC service with unstable code crashes, it wouldn't affect the main app's integrity.

As an additional benefit, XPC services can have their own entitlements. Such an approach allows developers to easily perform privilege separation for the application.

You can keep the main application sandboxed, while only a small portion of simple and reliable code will run out of the sandbox inside the XPC service.

This is only one example; it's up to the developer to separate privileges between multiple XPC services and the main app.

Consider using an XPC service in the following cases:

- To improve the stability of the app

- For proper privilege separation

- To explicitly split the app into the components

Install and Register

XPC services don't require any installation or registration process. They are always part of the application or framework. You just create one and use it. Simple!

Xcode has an explicit template called XPC Service to create such services, as shown in Figure 9-1.

Figure 9-1. *XPC Service target*

After you create the service, Xcode proposes to embed it into another target, as shown in Figure 9-2.

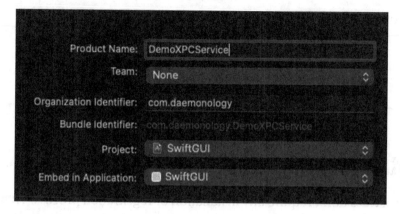

Figure 9-2. XPC service being embedded into another application

XPC Service's Info.plist

An XPC service has an interesting key that could be specified in its `Info.plist`:

`ServiceType <string> (default: Application)`

The type of the XPC service specifies how the service is instantiated. The values are as follows:

- `Application`: Each application will have a unique instance of this service.

- `User`: There is one instance of the service process created for each user.

- `System`: There is one instance of the service process for the whole system. System XPC services are restricted to residing in system frameworks and must be owned by root.

XPC Communication

To communicate via XPC, just use the XPC service bundle identifier as an XPC service endpoint. It's straightforward and simple, as shown in Listing 9-1.

Listing 9-1. XPC Service XPC Communication Specifics

```
// ObjC
[[NSXPCConnection alloc] initWithServiceName:@"com.daemonology.
DemoXPCService"]
```

```
// Swift
NSXPCConnection(serviceName: "com.daemonology.DemoXPCService")
```

```
XPC Service should prepare XPC listener:
// ObjC
[NSXPCListener serviceListener]
```

```
// Swift
NSXPCListener.service()
```

CHAPTER 10

Login Items

In this chapter, we'll discuss a special kind of user agent called a *login item* and the API related to them.

Login items are user agents with additional specifics. They are more restricted but have an official API to manage them. Login items always complement their parent applications.

Login Item Specifics

A login item has the following attributes:

- Run as a specific user

- Usually multiple instances in the system (a process for one user)

- Part of the app

- Bundle application

- App Store compatible

Naming Conventions

A login item in macOS doesn't have any explicit naming conventions. You can just follow the same rules as for user agents.

© Volodymyr Vashurkin 2021
V. Vashurkin, *macOS Daemonology*, https://doi.org/10.1007/978-1-4842-7277-0_10

When to Use

A login item is a simple alternative way to deal with user agent functionality.
They can be used instead of classic user agents in situations like these:

- When using only the official public API

- To be compatible with App Store

- Only a basic and simple user agent needed

Install and Register

The supported approach when dealing with a login item is
`ServiceManagement.framework`.

Note   Login items installed using the Service Management
framework are not visible in System Preferences and can be removed
only using the application that installed them.

Installing a login item is similar to dealing with privilege helpers, but
much simpler.

There is only one function to work with login items:
`SMLoginItemSetEnabled`.

Login Item Installation Overview

Follow these steps:

1. Create a host application or use an existing one.

2. Create a login item application. Pick a usual
   application for the login item. Set either the
   `LSUIElement` or `LSBackgroundOnly` key in the `Info.`
   `plist` file of the login item.

3. Copy the login item. The login item app should be copied into the `Contents/Library/LoginItems` subfolder of the host application, as shown in Figure 10-1.

Figure 10-1. *Login item placement inside the host application*

4. Call `SMLoginItemSetEnabled` from the host application. The `SMLoginItemSetEnabled` function takes two arguments: the bundle identifier of the login item and a Boolean specifying the desired state.

Listing 10-1. SMLoginItemSetEnabled Example

```
import Cocoa
import ServiceManagement

@main
class AppDelegate: NSObject, NSApplicationDelegate {
    func applicationDidFinishLaunching(_ aNotification:
    Notification) {
        let identifier = "com.daemonology.DemoLoginItem"
```

```
        ///
        /// Pass true to start LoginItem application immediately.
        /// It will be scheduled to be started every time
        /// the user logs in.
        ///
        /// Passing false terminates the LoginItem application and
        /// indicates that it should no longer be launched
        /// when the user logs in.
        ///
        let success = SMLoginItemSetEnabled(identifier as
        CFString, true)
        print("SMLoginItemSetEnabled success: \(success).")
    }
}
```

Notes

Login items don't support launchd configuration customization.

When enabled, macOS automatically creates a predefined configuration plist for the login item and bootstraps it via launchd.

Deinstallation

Use SMLoginItemSetEnabled(identifier, false) and the renamed login item.

You cannot disable a login item if you don't have a copy of it inside the bundle.

Login Item Shared Usage

If multiple applications (for example, several applications from the same company) contain a helper application with the same bundle identifier, only the one with the greatest bundle version number is launched. Any of the applications that contain a copy of the helper application can enable and disable it.

Deprecated API

In addition, there is an old API to manage login items, through a "shared file list." This API is still alive, but is deprecated since macOS 10.11.

You can reach it by searching for entities from LaunchServices. framework (LSSharedFileListCreate, LSSharedFileListInsertItemURL, kLSSharedFileListSessionLoginItems).

Login items that were installed using a shared file list are visible in System Preferences; users have direct control over them. If you use this API, your login item can be disabled by the user, so any other application that communicates with it should have reasonable fallback behavior in case the login item is disabled.

XPC Communication

A login item can be accessed via XPC in the same way as a user agent. The difference is that there is no way to customize the launchd configuration of a login item.

Fortunately, when a login item is enabled, macOS creates an XPC endpoint that is exactly the same as its bundle ID. So, a login item can be accessed via this XPC endpoint. This is how you can figure out the exact XPC endpoint of your login item (or any other daemon). Run a command like print gui/501/com.daemonology.DemoLoginItem in the Terminal.

In the output, see the section called endpoints:

```
endpoints = {
    "com.daemonology.DemoLoginItem" = {
        port = 0x10242f
```

```
        active = 0
        managed = 1
        reset = 0
        hide = 0
    }
}
```

You might get an error like this:

```
Error Domain=NSCocoaErrorDomain Code=4099 "The connection
to service on pid 0 named com.daemonology.DemoLoginItem was
invalidated." UserInfo={NSDebugDescription=The connection
to service on pid 0 named com.daemonology.DemoLoginItem was
invalidated.}.
```

If you get this error, it could mean a few things.

- Your XPC connection setup is invalid.

- Your host app is sandboxed, but you aren't following
  the additional rules (described next).

- SMLoginItemSetEnabled has failed.

LoginItems and Sandbox (AppStore Compatible)

A login item is, probably, the only way to have daemon-like applications when you go to the Mac App Store.

Login items can be used instead of user agents as a shared process accessed by XPC to coordinate multiple apps from your organization.

This chapter will reveal how to use login items as part of sandboxed applications.

To make a login item to be compatible with a sandboxed host application, you must satisfy the following rules. (Do not forget to enable at least Development code signing to see if your login item + the sandbox + XPC works.)

App Sandbox Entitlement

The host app and login items must all be app sandboxed.

Ensure both have corresponding entitlements in their `.entitlements` files.

LoginItem Bundle Identifier

The bundle identifier of a login item must start with the team ID.

An example is `ABCDEFGH.com.daemonology.DemoLoginItem`.

LoginItem Filename

The documentation says that login items must have filenames that match their bundle identifiers.

So for a login item with the bundle identifier, `ABCDEFGH.com.daemonology.DemoLoginItem` should have a filename of `ABCDEFGH.com.daemonology.DemoLoginItem.app`.

You can follow this advice, but I haven't found that it works in practice.

So actually, your login item may have a usual name like `DemoLoginItem`.

Application Group Entitlement

To communicate with each other, both the host app and its login items must declare themselves to be part of the same *application group*. Application groups are managed using the `com.apple.security.application-groups` entitlement.

The value of this entitlement is an array of bundle identifier prefixes. Add an entry in this array that matches the bundle identifier of the login item.

```
<key>com.apple.security.application-groups</key>
<array>
    <string>$(TeamIdentifierPrefix)com.daemonology</string>
</array>
```

Unfortunately, just (TeamIdentifierPrefix) is not enough for the application group identifier.

Note About $(TeamIdentifierPrefix)

This variable resolves into ABCDEFGH. Pay attention that it already has . at the end.

So, your group will be like $(TeamIdentifierPrefix)com.daemonology. Do not put a dot between it and the next word.

Resources

You can find a sample project in DemoLoginItem that can be used with the Mac App Store at Daemonology/5-LoginItem. Do not forget to enable code signing!

Also, consider looking at the official Apple example related to XPC login items that are compatible with a sandbox: https://developer.apple.com/library/archive/samplecode/AppSandboxLoginItemXPCDemo/Introduction/Intro.html.

PART III

Talking to your daemons

Installing the daemon is only half of the job. Another part is interacting with it.

For communication between processes Apple introduces XPC: native IPC mechanism that allows acting with remote processes like with usual objects.

CHAPTER 11

XPC at a Glance

In this chapter, we'll provide an overview of XPC mechanisms and their main concepts, and we'll present the most typical use case.

XPC Basics

Cross Process Communication (XPC) is a lightweight mechanism for interprocess communication integrated with Grand Central Dispatch (GCD) and `launchd`.

XPC is designed as a native bidirectional way to exchange data. It follows a classic approach of data exchange over connection. It assumes that there is a server (listener) and multiple clients (connections).

Clients can find the services to connect to using different sets of identifiers, as listed here:

- *Service name*: Identifies embedded XPC services (see Chapter 9)

- *Mach name*: Identifies any other kind of daemons registered via `launchd`

- *Endpoint*: Opaque data type uniquely identifies the listener

It's important to note that the XPC connection cannot be established *directly* between two regular processes. (If you want to do so, visit `// LINK`.)

© Volodymyr Vashurkin 2021
V. Vashurkin, *macOS Daemonology*, https://doi.org/10.1007/978-1-4842-7277-0_11

The listener (server) side of XPC must be known to launchd.

That's why in the daemon configuration plist we specify a dictionary of keys called MachServices. This dictionary associates a set of XPC endpoints with a particular daemon.

```
<key>MachServices</key>
<dict>
    <key>com.daemonology.testd.version.xpc</key>
    <true/>
    <key>com.daemonology.testd.auth.xpc</key>
    <true/>
</dict>
```

On-Demand Nature

One of the XPC design principles is its on-demand nature. When the client creates the connection and sends some data over it, the following happens:

1. The client communicates via launchd and asks for a certain XPC endpoint.

2. launchd searches for a registered endpoint requested by the client.

3. If the service corresponding to the specific endpoint is not launched, launchd starts it.

4. When it's started, the service should start all the XPC listeners it maintains.

5. launchd connects the client connection and the service listener endpoints (mach_ports under the hood).

6. The service listener checks and sets up the incoming connection from the client.

7. The data sent by the client into the connection comes into the service listener.

Note that creating an XPC connection (without sending any data) itself does nothing.

XPC API

There are two ways to deal with the XPC API.

- *NSXPCConnection API*: This is an Objective-C API that provides a remote procedure call mechanism, allowing the client application to call methods on proxy objects that transparently relay those calls to the corresponding objects in the service, and vice versa.

- *XPC services API*: This C-based API provides basic messaging services between a client application and a service.

The book gives a high-level overview of XPC, so the rest of the chapters will be focused on the NSXPCConnection API family.

Note   Regardless of the type of API, the XPC concepts remain the same.

According to Apple, the NSXPCConnection API is part of the Foundation framework and is described in the NSXPCConnection.h header file. It consists of the following pieces:

- NSXPCConnection: This class represents the bidirectional communications channel between two processes. Both the application and the service have at least one connection object.

- NSXPCInterface: This class describes the expected programmatic behavior of the connection (what classes can be transmitted across the connection, what objects are exposed, and so on).

- NSXPCListener: This class listens for incoming XPC connections. Your service must create it and assign it a delegate object that conforms to the NSXPCListenerDelegate protocol.

- NSXPCListenerEndpoint: This class uniquely identifies an NSXPCListener instance and can be sent to a remote process using NSXPCConnection. This allows a process to construct a direct communication channel between two other processes that otherwise could not see one another.

The NSXPCConnection API automatically serializes data structures and objects for transmission and deserializes them on the other end. Calling a method on a remote object is like calling a method on a local object.

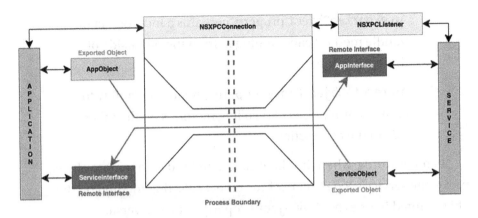

Figure 11-1. XPC communication overview

XPC communication requires the following:

– NSXPCInterface: This describes the connection behavior and provides the runtime information for connection. It uses the Objective-C protocol that describes what methods can be called from the remote process.

– NSXPCConnection object on both sides: On the service side, the connection is created by the XPC runtime and is coming into NSXPCListenerDelegate. On the client side, it should be created explicitly.

– NSXPCListener: This code in the service accepts and sets up incoming connections.

Each NSXPCConnection object provides three key features, as described here:

– An exportedInterface property describes the methods that should be made available to the opposite side of the connection.

109

- An exportedObject property contains a local object to handle method calls coming in from the other side of the connection.

- An remoteObjectProxy property provides an ability to obtain a proxy object for calling methods on the other side of the connection.

In other words, when the client calls a method on a remote object proxy, the service's NSXPCConnection object calls that method on the object stored in its exportedObject property, and vice versa.

NSXPCInterface

The NSXPCInterface describes the expected programmatic behavior of the connection. It is located on both sides of the XPC connection. It is always based on the Objective-C protocol.

Here is an example:

```
@objc(DAEServiceInterface)
protocol ServiceInterface {
    func uppercaseString(
        _ string: String,
        reply: @escaping (_ uppercased: String) -> Void
    )
}

let xpcInterface = NSXPCInterface(with: ServiceInterface.self)
```

Because of its asynchronous nature, XPC applies some limitations on the methods of the communication protocol.

The return type of the methods may be only Void or NSProgress (see Chapter 12).

To return the data, you can use a reply block. Any method may have only one parameter of the block type. Note that the reply block is one shot: it is expected to be called only once. Further calls will just do nothing.

Note   The reply block is a kind of asynchronous way of returning values from the functions/methods.

Where the usual (sync) function returns its result via the `return` statement, the `async` function returns its result, calling the passed-in callback (reply block) with the result.

Allowed types of all parameters to methods or reply blocks must be either of the following:

- Arithmetic types (`bool`, `int`, `char`, `float`, `double`, `uint64_t`, `NSUInteger`, and so on)

- C strings

- C structures and arrays containing only the types listed earlier

- Objective-C objects that implement the `NSSecureCoding` protocol (see Chapter 12)

- Objective-C protocols that represents proxy objects (see Chapter 12)

Client Side (NSXPCConnection)

The client side creates an instance of `NSXPCConnection` and sets it up.

Listing 11-1. XPC Communication, Client Side

```
// Create the connection. In this example, we create connection
to XPCService.
let connection = NSXPCConnection(serviceName: "com.daemonology.
TestXPC")

// setup the connection
connection.remoteObjectInterface = xpcInterface

// resume connection tells XPC runtime that connection is ready
to exchange the data
connection.resume()

// obtain remote proxy to perform a call
guard let proxy = connection.remoteObjectProxy as?
ServiceInterface else {
    fatalError("Invalid connection setup.")
}

// just call a method on proxy object like calling usual object
proxy.uppercaseString("lowercase string") { uppercased in
    print(uppercased)
}
```

Service Side (NSXPCListener)

Listing 11-2 shows the XPC communications.

Listing 11-2. XPC Communication, Listener (Server) Side

```
// Declaring Service object to work through XPC
class TheService: NSObject {}
```

```swift
// In this example, we'll use TheService as XPC exported object
// So it should conform to the exported interface.
extension TheService: ServiceInterface {
    func uppercaseString(
        _ string: String,
        reply: @escaping (String) -> Void
    ) {
        reply(string.uppercased())
    }
}

// Service side must have NSXPCListenerDelegate
extension TheService: NSXPCListenerDelegate {
    func listener(
        _ listener: NSXPCListener,
        shouldAcceptNewConnection newConnection:
        NSXPCConnection
    ) -> Bool {
        newConnection.exportedInterface = xpcInterface

        // use 'self' because TheService
        // conforms to 'ServiceInterface' protocol
        newConnection.exportedObject = self

        // resume the connection, telling XPC runtime
        // it is ready for handling messages
        newConnection.resume()

        // returning flag indicating if connection is accepted.
        return true
    }
}
```

```
let service = TheService()
let listener = NSXPCListener.service()
listener.delegate = service

// resuming the listener tells XPC runtime that
// listener is ready for handling connections.
listener.resume()
```

Handling Errors

This way of proxy object creation allows the user to specify an error handler for the exact proxy object.

```
remoteObjectProxyWithErrorHandler(_ handler: @escaping (Error)
-> Void) -> Any
```

A big advantage of such an approach is receiving errors during exact calls to the XPC.

The handler is not affected by any errors that are not related to this proxy object.

Interruption Handler

The handler is called when the process on the other end of the connection has crashed or has otherwise closed its connection.

The local connection object is usually still valid. Any future call will automatically trigger the service to be started again. It is safe to make new requests on the connection from an interruption handler.

Here are some notes:

- The behavior of the interruption handler is not actual for XPC connections created via NSXPCListenerEndpoint.

- When another party crashes and starts again, anonymous XPC listeners are created with other endpoints, which makes the existing NSXPCListenerEndpoint not valid.

- In such a case, you should request an updated NSXPCListenerEndpoint and create new connections.

Invalidation Handler

The handler is called when the invalidate method is called or when an XPC process could not be started. When this handler is called, the local connection object is no longer valid and must be re-created.

This is always the last handler called on a connection object. When this block is called, the connection object has been torn down. It is not possible to send further messages on the connection at that point, whether inside the handler or elsewhere in your code.

Troubleshooting

Here are some troubleshooting tips.

These are known XPC connection errors:

- NSXPCConnectionInterrupted = 4097

- NSXPCConnectionInvalid = 4099

- NSXPCConnectionReplyInvalid = 4101

Here are the known reasons for 4097:

- NSXPCInterface is a missing type used in the underlying protocol. Consider looking into Console.app for the appropriate XPC errors.

- Some custom types used for NSXPCInterface do not conform to NSSecureCoding.

- Some custom proxy protocol is not declared within NSXPCInterface.

Here are the known reasons for 4099:

- The service is not registered in launchd.

- The service invalidates the connection.

Resources

Consider reading the official Apple's documentation related to XPC services: https://developer.apple.com/library/archive/documentation/MacOSX/Conceptual/BPSystemStartup/Chapters/CreatingXPCServices.html.

Summary

In this chapter, we discussed the XPC mechanism design, XPC communication basics, and the API. We also covered the typical example of XPC use.

In the next chapters, we will dive into advances of XPC communication: passing custom object by copy, passing objects by proxy, and many more.

CHAPTER 12

Pass Objects by Copy Over XPC Using NSSecureCoding

In real-world scenarios, developers deal not with primitive types but with custom types that aggregate primitives. This chapter covers the topic of passing custom (aggregate) objects over XPC.

All objects passed over an NSXPC connection must conform to NSSecureCoding.

Apple provides such conforming for lots of classes such as NSString, NSURL, NSArray, NSImage, and so on.

But if you want to pass your own class over an XPC connection, you should conform to NSSecureCoding manually. Conforming to NSSecureCoding generally does not differ from NSCoding; see Listing 12-1.

Listing 12-1. Conforming to NSSecureCoding

```
@objc(DAECredentials)
public class Credentials: NSObject, NSSecureCoding, Codable {
    public var email: String
    public var serialNumber: Int
```

© Volodymyr Vashurkin 2021
V. Vashurkin, *macOS Daemonology*, https://doi.org/10.1007/978-1-4842-7277-0_12

```swift
public init(email: String, serialNumber: Int) {
    self.email = email
    self.serialNumber = serialNumber

    super.init()
}

// NSSecureCoding support
public static let supportsSecureCoding: Bool = true

public required init?(coder: NSCoder) {
    guard let email = coder.decodeObject(
            of: NSString.self,
            forKey: CodingKeys.email.stringValue
    ) else {
        return nil
    }

    self.email = email as String
    self.serialNumber = coder.decodeInteger(
        forKey: CodingKeys.serialNumber.stringValue
    )

    super.init()
}

public func encode(with coder: NSCoder) {
    coder.encode(email, forKey: CodingKeys.email.
    stringValue)
    coder.encode(serialNumber,
                forKey: CodingKeys.serialNumber.
                stringValue)
}
}
```

Note   In this example, classes may conform to the Codable protocol just to gain the ability of using the CodingKeys autogenerated enum. This helps to avoid copy-paste errors in encode/initWithCoder methods.

Collections

A special case is how to deal with collections such as arrays and dictionaries.

By design, collection types like NSArray and NSDictionary conform to NSSecureCoding. Passing objects over XPC requires them to be whitelisted for XPC. XPC automatically whitelists objects that appear in the method interface. But it does *not* whitelist custom classes that may appear inside the collections.

If a method of the XPC protocol contains a custom collection as a parameter, XPC runtime whitelists some types by default: NSDictionary, NSArray, NSSet, NSOrderedSet, NSData, NSString, NSDate, NSNumber, and NSNull.

This means that XPC will successfully encode/decode messages only if objects of the previous types will be passed into the method. Otherwise, XPC coding will fail. See Figure 12-1.

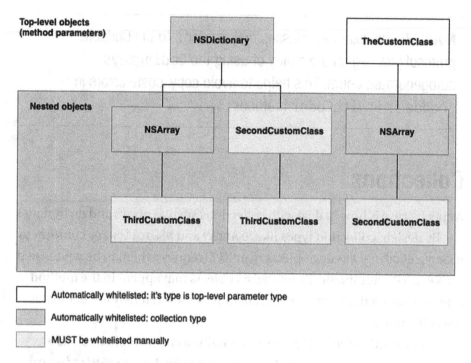

Figure 12-1. Whitelisting custom classes for XPC

Manual Whitelisting

Let's define the Objective-C protocol to play around.

```
@objc(DAETheCustomClass)
class TheCustomClass: NSObject, NSSecureCoding {}

@objc
protocol ServiceInterface {
    func foo(_ param1: String, _ param2: TheCustomClass)
    func bar(_ param: [TheCustomClass])
    func baz(_ convert: String, reply: @escaping
    (TheCustomClass) -> Void)
}
```

The class whitelisting is performed by the NSXPCInterface:

```
- (void)setClasses:(NSSet<Class> *)classes forSelector:(SEL)sel
argumentIndex:(NSUInteger)arg ofReply:(BOOL)ofReply;
- (NSSet<Class> *)classesForSelector:(SEL)sel
argumentIndex:(NSUInteger)arg ofReply:(BOOL)ofReply;
```

Let's investigate whitelisted classes for our interface.

Note: The setClasses API takes a few strange arguments. Let's take a closer look at them.

- forSelector: This is the method on the protocol to affect.

- argumentIndex: This is the 0-based index of the method's argument to make changes. For example, if we want to set classes for the param2 of the foo method, we will pass 1 as the argument index.

- ofReply: The reply block has its own numbering of arguments. Pass true if the argument we are going to affect is in the trailing reply block. See Listing 12-2.

Listing 12-2. Classes, Whitelisted for XPC by Default

```
let iface = NSXPCInterface(with: ServiceInterface.self)
print(iface.classes(
        for: #selector(ServiceInterface.foo),
        argumentIndex: 0, // the first parameter of
        ofReply: false    // ServiceInterface.foo method
) as NSSet)
// output: { NSString }

print(iface.classes(
        for: #selector(ServiceInterface.foo),
        argumentIndex: 1, // the second parameter of
```

```
        ofReply: false      // ServiceInterface.foo method
) as NSSet)
// output: { DAETheCustomClass }
```

```
print(iface.classes(
        for: #selector(ServiceInterface.baz),
        argumentIndex: 0, // the first parameter of
        ofReply: true      // ServiceInterface.baz method reply
                              block
) as NSSet)
// output: { TheCustomClass }
```

```
print(iface.classes(
        for: #selector(ServiceInterface.bar),
        argumentIndex: 0, // the first parameter of
        ofReply: false     // ServiceInterface.bar method
) as NSSet)
// output: { NSOrderedSet, NSSet, NSArray, NSString, NSData,
NSDate, NSNumber, NSDictionary, NSNull }
```

Note that the output for the bar method does not contain TheCustomClass by default.

We must whitelist it manually, as shown in Listing 12-3.

Listing 12-3. Manual Class Whitelisting

```
iface.setClasses(
    NSSet(array: [NSArray.self, TheCustomClass.self]) as Set,
    for: #selector(ServiceInterface.bar),
    argumentIndex: 0,
    ofReply: false
)
```

Important Note   When performing `setClasses`, you must declare *all* classes manually without relying on that XPC will keep the default set of classes like `NSArray`, `NSDictionary`, `NSString`, and so on.

You must also declare all nested classes of the custom type, even if they are default like `NSString`. Otherwise, XPC encode/decode will fail.

To prove this, just print classes after `setClasses`:

`{ NSArray, DAETheCustomClass }`

Security Consideration: Own Type That Contains a Collection

Decode collection classes safely.

Assume the custom class you are going to pass over XPC contains a nested array/dictionary of objects.

In the `initWithCoder:` method, when decoding the collection object or objects, always use `NSCoder`'s `decodeObjectOfClasses:forKey:` and provide a list of any objects that can appear within the collection.

Summary

In this chapter, we discussed and learned how to pass custom objects by copy over an XPC connection.

But what if the object is not designed to be copied and should just perform particular actions?

The next chapter covers passing objects by proxy.

CHAPTER 13

Pass Objects by Proxy: The Callable XPC Objects

In most cases, passing objects by copy is enough when exchanging data over XPC. Passing by copy is pretty straightforward, simple, and obvious and should be preferred when dealing with the NSXPC API.

But in some cases, passing by copy is not the way you want to communicate over XPC. In some cases, you want to pass some entities over a connection and use them as the usual callable objects, not like structs. The following are two examples:

- Progress reporting

- Delegating functionality to another process

The downside to passing objects by proxy is the performance penalty. It occurs because every access to the object requires interprocess communication.

For this reason, you should pass objects by proxy only if it is not possible to pass them by copy.

Proxy objects are configured in a similar way to dealing with the remoteObjectInterface property of the initial connection.

© Volodymyr Vashurkin 2021
V. Vashurkin, *macOS Daemonology*, https://doi.org/10.1007/978-1-4842-7277-0_13

```
@objc(DAEDemoXPCService)
protocol DemoXPCService {
    // Passing object by proxy.
    func download(resource: String, delegate: DownloadDelegate)
-> Void
}

@objc(DAEDownloadDelegate)
protocol DownloadDelegate {
    func downloadDidStart()
    func downloadDidUpdateProgress(downloaded: Int, total: Int)
    func downloadDidFinish(error: NSError?)
}
```

NSXPCInterface for the initial NSXPCConnection should be extended, as shown in Listing 13-1.

Listing 13-1. Introducing the Interface for the XPC Proxy Object

```
let interface = NSXPCInterface(with: DemoXPCService.self)

// Describe proxy object interface
let delegate = NSXPCInterface(with: DownloadDelegate.self)
interface.setInterface(
    delegate,
    for: #selector(DemoXPCService.download(resource:delegate:)),
    argumentIndex: 1, // the second parameter of
    ofReply: false    // download(resource:delegate:) method
)
```

After that, it is safe to pass any object of type NSObject that conforms to DownloadDelegate over an XPC connection. See Listing 13-2.

Listing 13-2. Example: Passing an Object by Proxy

```swift
// Client side
private class Client: NSObject {
//    ...

    func download() {
        let connection = NSXPCConnection(serviceName: "com.
        daemonology.DemoAdvancedXPC")

        let iface = NSXPCInterface(with: DemoXPCService.self)
        connection.remoteObjectInterface = iface
        connection.resume()

        let proxy = connection.remoteObjectProxy as!
        DemoXPCService
        proxy.download(resource: "this.book", delegate: self)
    }
}

extension Client: DownloadDelegate {
//    ...

    func downloadDidStart() {
        print("Download started")
    }

    func downloadDidUpdateProgress(downloaded: Int, total: Int) {
        print("Downloaded \(downloaded) from \(total)")
    }
```

```swift
    func downloadDidFinish(error: NSError?) {
        print("Download finished. Error: \(error).")
    }
}

// Service side
func download(resource: String, delegate: DownloadDelegate) {
    let parts = 5
    DispatchQueue.global().async {
        delegate.downloadDidStart()
        for i in 1...parts {
            sleep(1)
            delegate.downloadDidUpdateProgress(downloaded: i,
            total: parts)
        }
        delegate.downloadDidFinish(error: nil)
    }
}
```

NSProgress: Alternate Observation Mechanism Over XPC

Usually when dealing with XPC, we use asynchronous methods that return Void and provide results in their reply blocks.

macOS 10.13 changes this rule. Since 10.13, it is legal to return an NSProgress instance from the methods used by XPC as a return value with no additional setup, as shown in Listing 13-3.

Listing 13-3. Example: Returning NSProgress from XPC Method

```
@objc(DAEServiceInterface)
protocol ServiceInterface {
    func count(
        to n: Int,
        delay: TimeInterval,
        completion: @escaping () -> Void
    ) -> Progress
}
// Client side
let connection = NSXPCConnection(serviceName: "com.daemonology.
DemoAdvancedXPC")

let iface = NSXPCInterface(with: ServiceInterface.self)
connection.remoteObjectInterface = iface
connection.resume()

let proxy = connection.remoteObjectProxy as! ServiceInterface
let progress = proxy.count(to: 5, delay: 1) {
    print("Completed")
}
token = progress.observe(\.completedUnitCount) { p, _ in
    print("\(p.completedUnitCount) of \(p.totalUnitCount)")
}

// output
// 1 of 5
// 2 of 5
// 3 of 5
// 4 of 5
// 5 of 5
// Completed
```

Summary

In this chapter, we covered the most common and widespread approaches of XPC communication: passing objects by copy, passing objects by proxy, and reporting using NSProgress over XPC.

But there is one thing we have still not discussed: how to pass one XPC endpoint to another to allow direct communication between them. The next chapter is about that.

CHAPTER 14

NSXPCListener Endpoint: XPC Service Sharing

In this chapter, we will discuss how to share entire XPC services with each other over a direct connection. You can find samples at `Daemonology/ 7-NSXPCListenerEndpoint`.

You're already implemented a solution consisting of multiple daemons, services, and apps. At some point, you will want to use the functionality of one service in another. Let's look at an example: assume that communication is required between the service of a daemon and the service of an app. See Figure 14-1.

© Volodymyr Vashurkin 2021
V. Vashurkin, *macOS Daemonology*, https://doi.org/10.1007/978-1-4842-7277-0_14

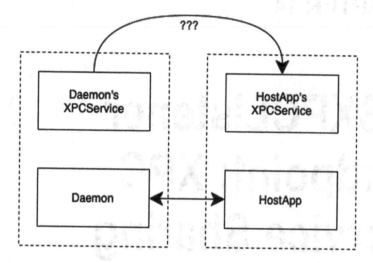

Figure 14-1. *Required communication schema*

Complexity of Passing by Proxy

One way to implement this functionality is to use proxy objects. But there are some cases of sharing functionality from service to service over a proxy. See Figure 14-2.

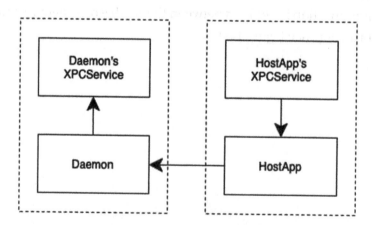

Figure 14-2. *Complexity of passing objects by proxy*

Here are the details:

- *Extra dependencies*: As shown in Figure 14-2, if the daemon's XPCService wants to communicate with HostApp's XPCService, all the intermediate components should declare the corresponding XPCInterface, etc., to forward the proxy object messages to all the applications. From an architectural point of view, this should be avoided.

- *Complexity of debugging and error handling*: If an error occurs somewhere in this connection schema, it is tricky to find where it is exactly. And if an error appears in the middle process, how should it be handled?

- *Performance costs*: XPC communication requires some extra work to deal with messages passed over a connection.

  Each XPC message is encoded in a special way into xpc_message, transmitted over a connection, and decoded on another side.

  For this case, that will require three encodings/decodings for each XPC message when only one is actually needed. See Figure 14-3.

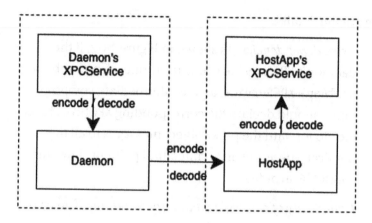

Figure 14-3. *Extra encodings/decodings*

There is no problem if there is not much communication, but if, for example, HostApp's XPCService represents a communication layer and the daemon's XPCService wants to send a lot of data over it, you'll run into big performance issues.

NSXPCListenerEndpoint to the Rescue

But wait. It seems this problem has been solved somewhere else...

Yep. That is how the launchd daemon helps to establish XPC communication; all roads end up in launchd. See Figure 14-4.

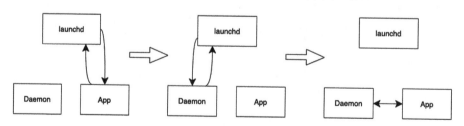

Figure 14-4. *XPC connection establishment*

The main idea is to have some endpoint descriptor that uniquely identifies the endpoint and allows you to establish an XPC connection to that endpoint directly.

Note   Regarding the endpoint descriptor, you may treat the descriptor (or handle) as some opaque type that is understandable for the system internals but has no sense to the outer world.

For example, file descriptors (fd) are just int values, but they are understood by the system calls like read/write.

At the same time, the descriptor is universal for the outer code (always the same type), but for the internal system, the descriptor may be processed in a different way. As an example, the file descriptor may refer to a file, socket, or any other resource.

The XPC API provides such an approach: using NSXPCListenerEndpoint.

On the service side, you create an anonymous NSXPCListener and get its endpoint.

On the client side, you create NSXPCConnection using some listener endpoint. See Listing 14-1.

Listing 14-1. Establish Anonymous XPC Connection

```
// Server side (accepts connections)
let listener = NSXPCListener.anonymous()
let endpoint = listener.endpoint
```

```
// Client side (connects the server)
let connection = NSXPCConnection(listenerEndpoint: endpoint)
```

NSXPCListenerEndpoint allows you to connect even independent XPC services with each other just by passing an endpoint instance over existing XPC connections from one service to another.

This approach allows you to avoid unnecessary encodings/decodings and dependencies across all of your product ecosystem.

XPC Service Testability

The anonymous NSXPCListener and NSXPCListenerEndpoint also provide the ability to mock the entire XPC service for testing purposes.

Imagine you have a class that performs its job of connecting the XPC service and dealing with it.

Initially, this kind of dependency requires the XPC service to run and perform real-world tasks and acts like external dependencies for that class.

When designing your services, you may want to implement some internal functionality to let one side of your system get an instance of NSXPCListener or NSXPCConnection from the outside instead of creating ones inside the system.

Then, in tests, you can just pass the local anonymous listener or its endpoint and perform some expectations/mocks on the other end.

Summary

In the previous chapters, we learned all about communication over XPC using the NSXPC API.

Now it is time to speak about XPC security: you don't want a hacker to access your private XPC endpoint, do you?

CHAPTER 15

XPC Security

In this chapter, we will discuss some recommendations related to securing the XPC communication between processes based on code signing.

Assume your app is split into the main application and the privileged helper that performs root actions. You have users who trust you and install your software and grant it admin privileges.

But you forgot to secure the XPC connection between the main application and the privileged helper. In this case, a bad guy can use your privileged helper to perform malicious actions.

What's the Problem?

XPC communication between processes is a cool thing. You are allowed to split your application into multiple services, connect some of them with elevated privileges, and join them into one product.

But how do you restrict the XPC communication to only the desired processes?

Usually we want to exchange data and perform actions only between our own services and no one else's.

An XPC connection by default has no checks on who is allowed to connect. So, anyone can reach the process over XPC if he knows the XPC endpoint name and remote/exported protocols.

Getting the XPC endpoint name is easy: a bad guy just investigates the daemon's configuration plist or print properties via the launchctl tool.

© Volodymyr Vashurkin 2021
V. Vashurkin, *macOS Daemonology*, https://doi.org/10.1007/978-1-4842-7277-0_15

Getting the remote/exported protocols is a bit harder but possible. A bad guy just needs to apply some reverse engineering techniques to get them.

As a result, anyone can use your daemons over XPC. The really bad situation is when your daemon has root privileges and the connection is not secured.

Fortunately, the XPC API provides some additional information about the other side of the connection to perform some security checks.

Protection Mechanism

NSXPCListenerDelegate can perform some security checks on connections and make some decisions.

```
func listener(_ listener: NSXPCListener,
shouldAcceptNewConnection newConnection: NSXPCConnection) ->
Bool
```

If the function returns false, the connection will be rejected.

So, the task of securing the XPC communication narrows to the single method where a decision is made if a connection is allowed.

To make a decision if a new connection is allowed or denied, we may use some properties of the incoming XPC connection. See Listing 15-1.

Listing 15-1. Some NSXPCConnection Properties

```
var auditSessionIdentifier: au_asid_t
var processIdentifier: pid_t
var effectiveUserIdentifier: uid_t
var effectiveGroupIdentifier: gid_t
```

In addition, NSXPCConnection provides some security attributes, which is really helpful for maybe only the PID of the incoming connection. But the latest security research (for example, see https://saelo.github.io/ presentations/warcon18_dont_trust_the_pid.pdf) shows that the PID is not secure enough.

As an alternative to a PID, to uniquely identify the process, macOS provides an audit token (audit_token_t). NSXPCConnection does not expose the audit token in a public API, but it can be retrieved using a simple private API. See Listing 15-2.

Listing 15-2. Accessing audit_token of NSXPCConnection

```
@interface NSXPCConnection(PrivateAuditToken)
@property (nonatomic, readonly) audit_token_t auditToken;
@end
```

XPC Security and Code Signature

Probably the best way to secure the connection is to evaluate the code signature of the incoming party. The code signature provides many useful properties, including the following:

- Verdict if the code signature is not broken

- Signing identity used to sign the application

- Team identifier of the signer

- Check of the codesign requirements

- Hardened runtime flag

- Applied entitlements

In a general case, the code signature can be obtained using a security framework. See Listing 15-3.

Listing 15-3. Obtaining Codesign Information with an Audit Token

```
// MARK: - SecCode

func copySelfCode() -> SecCode? { ... }
func copyTokenCode(_ token: audit_token_t) -> SecCode? { ... }

// MARK: - Codesign information

func copySigningInformation(for secCode: SecCode) -> [String:
Any]? {
    var secStaticCode: SecStaticCode!
    guard SecCodeCopyStaticCode(
            secCode,
            SecCSFlags(rawValue: 0),
            &secStaticCode
    ) == errSecSuccess else{
        print("Couldn't get SecStaticCode from the SecCode")
        return nil
    }

    var cfSigningInformation: CFDictionary!
    guard SecCodeCopySigningInformation(
        secStaticCode,
        SecCSFlags(
            rawValue: kSecCSSigningInformation |
                kSecCSDynamicInformation |
                kSecCSContentInformation
        ),
        &cfSigningInformation
    ) == errSecSuccess else {
        NSLog("Couldn't obtain signing information")
        return nil
    }
```

```
guard let signingInformation = cfSigningInformation as?
[String: Any] else {
    NSLog("Signing information dict has invalid format")
    return nil
}

return signingInformation
}
```

For example, for a simple test console application, the signing information is a dictionary with keys. See Listing 15-4.

Listing 15-4. Code Signature Information

```
"identifier": <NSString>
"main-executable": <NSURL>
"flags": <NSNumber>
"teamid": <NSString>
"signing-time": <NSDate>
"certificates": <NSArray>
"entitlements": <NSData>
"entitlements-dict": <NSDictionary>
"cms": <NSData>
"cdhashes": <NSArray>
"cdhashes-full": <NSDictionary>
"digest-algorithms": <NSArray>
"trust": <SecTrustRef>
"digest-algorithm": <NSNumber>
"changed-files": <NSArray>
"unique": <NSData>
"format": <NSString>
"source": <NSString>
```

Securing an XPC Connection

The simplest way to ensure that the client is signed with the same codesign identity as a service is to compare the signing team identifiers. See Listing 15-5.

Listing 15-5. Restricting XPC Communication to the Same Development Team

```
func listener(
    _ listener: NSXPCListener,
    shouldAcceptNewConnection newConnection: NSXPCConnection
    ) -> Bool {
    guard let selfCode = copySelfCode(),
        let selfSigningInfo = copySigningInformation(for:
        selfCode),
        let connectionCode = copyTokenCode(newConnection.
        auditToken),
        let connectionSigningInfo = copySigningInformation(for:
        connectionCode)
    else {
        return false
    }

    guard let selfTeamID = selfSigningInfo[kSecCodeInfoTeam
    Identifier as String] as? String,
        let connectionTeamID = connectionSigningInfo[kSecCode
        InfoTeamIdentifier as String] as? String
    else {
        return false
    }
```

```
newConnection.exportedInterface = ...
newConnection.exportedObject = ...
newConnection.resume()

return selfTeamID == connectionTeamID
}
```

SMJobBless and XPC Security

Additional attention should be given to the SMJobBless function that installs PrivilegedHelper into the system.

By design, SMJobBless requires codesign requirements to be specified for both the host application and the PrivilegedHelper itself (more about this can be found in Chapter 6).

This requirement is checked only once by the SMJobBless function and works only when PrivilegedHelper is installed on the system.

They does not secure the XPC connection to the privileged helper!

In short, this means that the XPC connection with PrivilegedHelper *must* be additionally secured (as described earlier in the chapter) like any other XPC connections.

Of course, information from the Info.plist key SMAuthorizedClients can be also used to authorize incoming connections.

Exceptions in XPC Connection Security

For the best level of security, ideally you should always protect your XPC connections. In the real world, in some cases the XPC communication can be left in an unprotected state and still be secure.

XPC Service

In most cases, applications deal with their own XPC services, and launchd spawns a new XPC service process for each application that reaches it. This means nobody else can connect to your private XPC service via XPC.

In such cases, you can skip any security checks.

Warning   In rare cases, XPC services can be launched as a singleton for the user session or whole system. This behavior is controlled by a specific key in the Info.plist file of the XPC service (see Chapter 9).

In such cases, additional considerations regarding XPC connection security should be made.

Public Functional

XPC security can be omitted if you are developing a service that can be accessed via any process in the system by design.

For example, it may be a sharing service, SDK, or something else that is designed to have anyone connect to it.

CHAPTER 16

XPC and Swift

In this chapter, we'll show how to adopt XPC communication using Swift (passing structures over XPC, working with callbacks instead of delegates, and so on). You can find a sample at `https://github.com/Alkenso/sXPC` called `sXPC_Sample`.

Lack of Swift Support

The NSXPC API mechanism is a great way for applications to communicate with each other. Initially, the NSXPC API was designed to deal with only the Objective-C language without any support for Swift.

Nowadays, Swift provides powerful features and possibilities. Some, such as complex enums and structures, are unfortunately not compatible with XPC. Also, the existing NSXPC API is not strict typed for remote/exported object proxies, which adds some complications and requires boilerplate code when dealing with Swift.

Proposed Approach: sXPC Library

While working on multiple projects, I've faced the inconvenience of mixing Swift code with the Objective-C oriented NSXPC API.

As a solution, I've created a Swift wrapper around the native Objective-C API (see Listing 16-1).

© Volodymyr Vashurkin 2021
V. Vashurkin, *macOS Daemonology*, https://doi.org/10.1007/978-1-4842-7277-0_16

sXPC allows you to do the following:

- Make NSXPCConnection produce the typed remoteObject and set a typed exportedObject.

- Pass Swift-only structs/enums over an XPC connection (with very little additional code).

- Have the NSXPCInterface description in a single place.

- Hide the Objective-C details, using pure Swift across the application codebase.

Listing 16-1. Swift XPC API

```
// Assume protocol you are going to use over XPC connection
public struct Request: Equatable, Codable {
    public var processUID: uid_t
    public var processPID: pid_t
    public var processPath: URL
}

public struct Response: Equatable, Codable {
    public var allow: Bool
    public var cache: Bool
}

public protocol Service {
    func perform(
        _ request: Request,
        reply: @escaping (Response) -> Void)
}

// Create connection & call
let connection = CreateServiceXPCConnection(connection:
NSXPCConnection(serviceName: "com.example.XPCService"))
connection.resume()
```

```
// proxy is entity of Service, pure Swift protocol
let proxy = connection.remoteObjectProxy { error in
    print(error)
}

let request = Request(...)
proxy.perform(request) { response in print(response) }
```

// Setup the listener
```
let listener = CreateServiceXPCListener(listener: listener)
```

```
// Closure-based instead of delegate-based
listener.newConnectionHandler = {
    $0.exportedObject = DummyService()
    $0.resume()
    return true
}
listener.resume()
```

Next, let's reveal how the code implements all of that magic.

Swift XPC API Internals

Internally, the approach requires some glue code. First, we need an Objective-C compatible protocol that deals with the XPC runtime under the hood. In Swift we often use custom structures, classes, and enums that are unknown to Objective-C. For such cases, we need to write some boilerplate (but template) code to bridge these custom elements into Objective-C classes.

Last but not least, we need to implement the Objective-C protocol to work with the Swift protocol, and vice versa. Usually they are pretty small but important.

The beautiful thing is that we can implement all of this bridging code in a module-internal manner without exposing any implementation details to the outside world. Listing 16-2 shows the first step of using an underlying Objective-C compatible protocol.

Listing 16-2. Bridging an Objective-C Compatible Protocol

```
@objc
protocol ServiceXPC {
    func perform(_ request: Request.XPC, reply: @escaping
    (Response.XPC) -> Void)
}
```

Listing 16-3 shows the second step of putting wrappers around the pure-Swift types.

Listing 16-3. Bridging Pure-Swift Types

```
extension Request {
    typealias XPC = RequestXPC
    var xpcValue: XPC { XPC(value: self) }
}

/// Underlying Obj-C compatible class backed up 'Request' type
    NSXPCConnection.
/// - note: If the file is not in the shared framework but
    linked to multiple targets, name it explicitly like
    @objc(CCRequestXPC).
class RequestXPC: NSObject, NSSecureCoding {
    typealias Wrapped = Request
    let value: Wrapped
```

```
required init(value: Wrapped) {
    self.value = value
    super.init()
}

static var supportsSecureCoding: Bool = true

func encode(with coder: NSCoder) {
    coder.encodeCodable(value)
}

required convenience init?(coder: NSCoder) {
    guard let value = coder.decodeCodable() as Wrapped?
    else { return nil }
    self.init(value: value)
}
}
```

Listing 16-4 shows the next step of implementing the bridging between Objective-C and Swift. The XPCInterface entity of the sXPC library gathers all the runtime and bridging code.

Listing 16-4. Creation of sXPC Wrappers

```
func CreateServiceXPCInterface() -> XPCInterface<Service,
ServiceXPC> {
    class ToXPC: NSObject, ServiceXPC {
        let instance: Service
        init(_ instance: Service) { self.instance = instance }
        func perform(_ request: Request.XPC, reply: @escaping
        (Response.XPC) -> Void) {
            instance.perform(request.value, reply: {
            reply($0.xpcValue) })
        }
    }
```

```
struct FromXPC: Service {
    let proxy: ServiceXPC
    func perform(_ request: Request, reply: @escaping
    (Response) -> Void) {
        proxy.perform(request.xpcValue, reply: {
        reply($0.value) })
    }
}

let interface = NSXPCInterface(with: ServiceXPC.self)
return XPCInterface(interface: interface, toXPC:
ToXPC.init, fromXPC: FromXPC.init)
}
```

Index